GREAT SPORTS TEAMS

THE CHICAGO BULLS

JOHN F. GRABOWSKI

LUCENT BOOKS
SAN DIEGO, CALIFORNIA

THOMSON
─────★─────™
GALE

Detroit • New York • San Diego • San Francisco
Boston • New Haven, Conn. • Waterville, Maine
London • Munich

Library of Congress Cataloging-in-Publication Data

Grabowski, John F.
    Chicago Bulls / by John F. Grabowski.
        p. cm. — (Great sports teams)
Summary: Discusses the history, formation, development,
and popularity of the Chicago Bulls basketball team,
including a look at individual players who have had an
impact on the success of the team.
Includes bibliographical references and index.
    ISBN 1-56006-937-6 (hbk. : alk. paper)
    1. Chicago Bulls (Basketball team)—History—Juvenile
literature. [1. Chicago Bulls (Basketball team)—History. 2.
Basketball—History.] I. Title. II. Series.
    GV885.52.C45 G73 2003
    796.323′64′0977311—dc21

2002000451

Copyright 2003 by Lucent Books,
an imprint of The Gale Group
10911 Technology Place, San Diego, California 92127

Contents

FOREWORD

Former Supreme Court Chief Justice Warren Burger once said he always read the sports section of the newspaper first because it was about humanity's successes, while the front page listed only humanity's failures. Millions of people across the country today would probably agree with Burger's preference for tales of human endurance, record-breaking performances, and feats of athletic prowess. Although these accomplishments are far beyond what most Americans can ever hope to achieve, average people, the fans, do want to affect what happens on the field of play. Thus, their role becomes one of encouragement. They cheer for their favorite players and team and boo the opposition.

ABC Sports president Roone Arledge once attempted to explain the relationship between fan and team. Sport, said Arledge, is "a set of created circumstances—artificial circumstances—set up to frustrate a man in pursuit of a goal. He has to have certain skills to overcome those obstacles—or even to challenge them. And people who don't have those skills cheer him and admire him." Over a period of time, the admirers may develop a rabid— even irrational—allegiance to a particular team. Indeed, the word "fan" itself is derived from the word "fanatic," someone possessed by an excessive and irrational zeal. Sometimes this devotion to a team is because of a favorite player; often it's because of where a person lives, and, occasionally, it's because of a family allegiance to a particular club.

4

Whatever the reason, the bond formed between team and fan often defies reason. It may be easy to understand the appeal of the New York Yankees, a team that has gone to the World Series an incredible thirty-eight times and won twenty-six championships, nearly three times as many as any other major league baseball team. It is more difficult, though, to comprehend the fanaticism of Chicago Cubs fans, who faithfully follow the progress of a team that hasn't won a World Series since 1908. Regardless, the Cubs have surpassed the 2 million mark in home attendance in fourteen of the last seventeen years. In fact, their two highest totals were posted in 1999 and 2000, when the team finished in last place.

Each volume in Lucent's *Great Sports Teams in History* series examines a team that has left its mark on the "American sports consciousness." Each book looks at the history and tradition of the club in an attempt to understand its appeal and the loyalty —even passion—of its fans. Each volume also examines the lives and careers of people who played significant roles in the team's history. Players, managers, coaches, and front-office executives are represented.

Endnoted quotations help bring the text in each book to life. In addition, all books include an annotated bibliography and a For Further Reading list to supply students with sources for conducting additional individual research.

No one volume can hope to explain fully the mystique of the New York Yankees, Boston Celtics, Dallas Cowboys, or Montreal Canadiens. The Lucent *Great Sports Teams in History* series, however, gives interested readers a solid start on the road to understanding the mysterious bond that exists between modern professional sports teams and their devoted followers.

INTRODUCTION

A Town Hungry for a Winner

In 1951, columnist A.J. Liebling wrote a three-part series for the *New Yorker* titled "Chicago: The Second City." It was a derisive profile of what was, at the time, the nation's second largest metropolis. In it, he found Chicago inferior in every aspect, from fashion to baseball to restaurants, when compared to his native New York. The "Second City" nickname has stuck with the town ever since.

One area in which the city has taken a backseat to others in recent times is professional sports. In football, the Bears were a force in years gone by but have struggled recently. Likewise, hockey's Blackhawks have not won the Stanley Cup since 1961. In baseball, the Cubs and White Sox have become symbols of futility. Neither club has played in the World Series over the past forty years, and neither has won a championship in more than three-quarters of a century. In addition, the infamous Chicago Black Sox brought shame to the city by throwing the World Series to the Cincinnati Reds in 1919.

With such a history of mediocrity, it is easy to understand why Chicago met the birth of the Bulls in 1966 with a less-than-enthusiastic response. Professional basketball had been on the

Chicago scene since the 1920s. The sport was mostly a regional phenomenon until the emergence of the Basketball Association of America (BAA), the forerunner of the National Basketball Association (NBA), in 1946. The Chicago Stags were a charter member of the BAA, but folded in 1950. The team failed to capture the city's interest, so there was no reason to think the Bulls would be any different.

The Bulls stumbled along in mediocrity for nearly two decades before that fateful day in 1984 when they selected Michael Jordan in the college draft. When fans had a chance to see the magic he could perform on the court, they realized they were watching

Michael Jordan celebrates after winning the NBA Championship in 1998. Jordan helped catapult the Chicago Bulls to fame after he joined the team in 1984.

someone special. The Second City was now home to arguably the greatest basketball player the game had ever seen. When management began to surround Jordan with better players who complemented his skills, the team emerged as a force to be reckoned with. The Bulls put together one of the greatest streaks in basketball history, winning six national championships over a span of eight years.

Not only did the Bulls make their mark as one of the league's all-time greatest teams, they also helped the NBA achieve international recognition. League commissioner David Stern tells the story of the time he visited China in 1991. A young boy approached him near the Great Wall and asked, in broken English, "How are the Red Oxen?"[1] Puzzled at first, Stern soon realized that "oxen" could be translated as "bulls" and that the red referred to the color on the Chicago Bulls logo. This teenager thousands of miles from Chicago was a fan of the Chicago Bulls.

There was probably no sports team more recognizable anywhere in the world than the Chicago Bulls of the 1990s. The team's tremendous appeal transcended national and racial boundaries. After decades of mediocrity, the Second City finally had a sports team that was second to none.

CHAPTER 1

Making the Most of a Third Chance

Professional basketball began to gain a toehold nationally in the mid-1940s. Prior to that, it had been mostly a regional phenomenon, with leagues centered in various parts of the country. The Basketball Association of America, the forerunner of the National Basketball Association, did not come into existence until 1946. By 1961, the eight-team NBA had become established enough to warrant thoughts of expansion. Since Chicago was the largest city in the nation not represented in the league (the Chicago Stags had been a charter member of the BAA, but folded in 1950), it was a natural choice for a franchise. In 1961, the Chicago Packers joined the league, playing their home games in the Chicago Amphitheatre.

Despite headliner Walt Bellamy, the league's Rookie of the Year, the Packers finished with a league-worst record of 18-62. The team had difficulty drawing fans, so owner Dave Trager sold it to a group who wanted to move the club to Baltimore. Yet, the arena being planned was not going to be ready until 1963, so the team had to play one more year in Chicago. The club, renamed the Zephyrs, managed to win only twenty-five games. The next year, they became the Baltimore Bullets and Chicago was again without

Walt Bellamy of the Chicago Zephyrs leaps for a rebound in a game against the New York Knicks in 1962.

a team. Having twice failed to support a pro team, the Windy City's prospects for a third franchise did not appear bright. However, Chicago was soon given another opportunity when the Bulls were formed in 1966. This time the team would not only last but would become one of basketball's greatest teams.

The Birth of the Bulls

When Trager was looking for buyers for his team, one of the people who had expressed interest was Chicago businessman Dick Klein. Klein wanted to keep the team in Chicago but was unable to raise the necessary funds. "My pockets just weren't deep enough,"[2] he would later recount. He did not give up his dream, however, and when the league decided to expand once more, he made his move.

This time, Klein had more than enough financial backing. The problem was that the league was not anxious to locate a new team in a city that had failed to support one just a short time before. Luckily for Klein, the American Broadcasting Company (ABC) was in the middle of negotiating a television contract with the NBA. Roone Arledge, head of ABC Sports, told the league it needed a team in Chicago in order to raise the advertising revenue that would make the venture a success.

Thanks to ABC's influence, Chicago was again in the running for a team. On January 26, 1966, Klein made his presentation before the NBA Board of Governors. As he later recalled, "I said, 'I have approximately a half-dozen partners, and any one of them could buy the whole league. So we have financial stability and we're in it for the long haul.'"[3] The NBA was convinced. The Chicago Bulls would open the 1966–1967 season as the league's tenth team.

Growing Pains

One of Klein's first moves was to decide on a coach. He chose Johnny "Red" Kerr, a Chicago native and former University of Illinois basketball star who was at the tail end of his career as an NBA player. Klein saw the quick-witted Kerr as the perfect choice, someone who could remain upbeat and entertain the media as the team went through its growing pains. Kerr's reason for accepting the position was partly selfish. "One of the reasons I wanted to coach the Bulls," he said, "is because I was born and raised here. . . . I wanted to be part of the team staying in Chicago so that when I was done playing and coaching, I could still go to see an NBA game in my town."[4]

Klein also hired Kerr's longtime friend, Philadelphia 76ers guard Al Bianchi, as the league's first full-time assistant coach. Since both Kerr and Bianchi were still under playing contracts, Klein had to select them as players in the expansion draft that was set up to stock the new team.

The eighteen players selected by the Bulls were Kerr and Jerry Sloan from the Baltimore Bullets; Ron Bonham and John Thompson from the Boston Celtics; Nate Bowman and Tom Thacker from the Cincinnati Royals; John Barnhill and Don Kojis from the

Detroit Pistons; Bob Boozer and Jim King from the Los Angeles
Lakers; Len Chappell and Barry Clemens from the New York
Knicks; Bianchi and Gerry Ward from the Philadelphia 76ers; Jeff
Mullins and Jim Washington from the St. Louis Hawks; and
Keith Erickson and McCoy McLemore from the San Francisco
Warriors. Before the season started, the Bulls added veteran
guard Guy Rodgers from the Warriors in a trade for Mullins and
King. They also added rookies Dave Schellhase and Erwin
Mueller, who were selected in the college draft. The Bulls were
now ready to open the season.

A Surprising Start

No one expected the Bulls to do well in their maiden season.
Therefore, it was something of a surprise when they traveled to
St. Louis on October 15, 1966, and defeated the Hawks, 104-97, in
their first regular season game. The victory was particularly satisfying to the Bulls because of their opponent. As Kerr recalled,
"Richie Guerin, who was coaching St. Louis, had predicted before the season that we wouldn't win ten games, so that first victory was very sweet."[5]

Chicago fans, however, were not impressed. Only forty-two
hundred people showed up three days later at the team's home
opener in the Amphitheater to see the Bulls defeat the Warriors
by a 119-116 count. The club continued to surprise, winning its
next game and compiling a 7-6 record nearly a month into the
season. A nine-game losing streak followed, but the team
bounced back later in the year after an inspiring victory over the
Philadelphia 76ers on March 1. (The 76ers would win the league
championship, compiling an incredible 68-13 mark.) The Bulls
finished strongly and shocked everyone by qualifying for the
postseason playoffs with a 33-48 record. The wins were the most
ever for an NBA expansion team in its first season.

Reality set in during the playoffs. The team was swept in its
best-of-three Western Conference Semifinals series with the
Hawks. In recognition of the club's overall success in its first
season, however, Kerr was named the NBA Coach of the Year.
In addition, Sloan and Rodgers made the All-Star team, the
latter topping the league in assists with an average of 11.2 per
game.

Guy Rodgers grabs the ball in a 1967 game against the Philadelphia 76ers.
Rodgers left the San Francisco Warriors to join the Chicago Bulls.

After the team's surprising first-year accomplishments, the Bulls failed to show improvement in their second season. They lost fifteen of their first sixteen games; as a result, attendance fell. Forced to play their home games in the larger Chicago Stadium, they occasionally played before crowds of less than a thousand. Although they finished with a poorer record than their first season, the Bulls did manage to make the playoffs again. They even recorded their first postseason win in their series with the Lakers.

The relationship between Kerr and the owners, however, showed signs of strain. Kerr objected to Klein's involvement in basketball matters and eventually resigned to become coach of the expansion Phoenix Suns. To take his place, Klein reached into the college ranks and hired little-known Dick Motta of Weber State in Utah. Although he was unknown, Motta had won three Big Sky Conference championships in his years with the school.

The Motta Years

It did not take long for Motta to clash with Klein over Klein's involvement in team affairs. When Klein sold center Erwin Mueller in order to increase cash flow, Motta exploded. "You can't play money," he announced to the media, throwing a dollar bill on the Chicago Stadium floor. "Money won't play."[6] With attendance down, rumors of the Bulls' relocation to another city began to circulate.

The Bulls finished Motta's first year as coach with a record of 33-49, missing the playoffs for the first time in their history. The high point of the season proved to be a November trade with Milwaukee. The Bulls sent high-scoring guard Flynn Robinson to the Bucks in exchange for guard Bob Weiss and forward Bob Love. The pair would play significant roles in the team's improvement over the next couple of years.

The 1969–1970 season brought some structural changes. Upset at Klein's rift with Motta, the rest of the Bulls' ownership group ousted Klein as the team's president. Former 76ers promotions whiz Pat Williams was hired as general manager. With Chicago, he continued his magic. He hired someone to be the team mascot, Benny the Bull, and ran numerous promotions to bring fans to Chicago Stadium. On the court, he improved the club by obtaining high-scoring forward Chet Walker from Philadelphia.

Williams' efforts were successful. The Bulls averaged better than ten thousand fans per home game for the first time in their history and finished with a 39-43 record. They lost to the Hawks in the first round of the playoffs, but it was obvious they were headed in the right direction.

Motta incorporated a style of play that used a set, patterned offense, or in other words many diagrammed plays. Forwards Walker and Love did the bulk of the scoring. Guard Sloan and center Tom Boerwinkle hounded opponents with their hard-nosed defense. As a result, the team reached the fifty-win mark for the first time in 1970–1971. Motta was named Coach of the Year for his contribution, and Love set a franchise single-season scoring record with 2,043 points.

The Bulls continued their solid play over the next three seasons, using one of the league's best defenses to win fifty-seven, fifty-one, and fifty-four games. They accomplished this despite several changes in the front office. In 1972, Arthur Wirtz took over as principal owner of the team, bringing a more business-like atmosphere to the organization. Complimentary and discount tickets, for example, were eliminated. The following year, Williams resigned as general manager after repeated confrontations with Motta. By this point, Motta was in complete control of the team, handling all the responsibilities of coach, general manager, and scout.

Despite the club's success, it had not yet managed to get past the second round of the playoffs. After a 47-35 season in 1974–1975, the Bulls missed their chance to get to the finals for the first time by losing their series with the Golden State Warriors after having taken a three-games-to-two lead. With the nucleus of his team getting older, Motta knew they had blown their best chance. The next year, Walker retired after a bitter salary dispute and Sloan suffered a serious knee injury. The Bulls' record fell to a league-worst 24-58. Following the end of the season, Motta resigned.

Former Bulls coach Dick Motta applauds on the sidelines. Motta was named Coach of the Year during the 1970–1971 season.

Musical Coaches

After a period of relative stability with Motta in charge, the Bulls embarked on an eight-year period that saw eight coaches take over the reins of the team. Former assistant coach Ed Badger guided the club to a strong finish in 1976–1977 in what became known as the "Miracle on Madison." With a team built around former American Basketball Association (ABA) star Artis Gilmore, the Bulls won twenty of their last twenty-four games to finish tied for second in the Midwest Division. "That's probably my fondest memory of my years with the Bulls," remembered Gilmore. "It created a major excitement within the city."[7] Attendance for the year reached a franchise-high 13,386 per game.

In the playoffs, Chicago lost a tough series to the eventual champions, the Portland Trail Blazers. Portland coach Jack Ramsay later said, "The Bulls were our toughest series that year. Fortunately, we had home-court advantage."[8]

Unfortunately for Chicago, the playoff run was just a tease. The Bulls had just one winning season over the next seven years. Despite the continued all-star play of Gilmore, injuries, mediocre drafts, and poor team chemistry combined to drag the club down. In succeeding years, Larry Costello, Scotty Robertson, Jerry Sloan, Phil Johnson, Rod Thorn, Paul Westhead, and Kevin Loughery followed Badger at the helm. None could turn the team's fortunes around, although the club did make the playoffs in 1980–1981 under Sloan.

Bad luck also added to the mix. Just prior to the 1979 college draft, the Bulls lost a coin flip with the Lakers for the right to the first pick. With that pick, the Lakers selected future All-Star Earvin "Magic" Johnson. The Bulls had to settle for UCLA's David Greenwood, who, although a respectable pro, was not in Johnson's class.

The 1983–1984 season marked a low point for the club. The Bulls finished the year with a record of 27-55, the second worst mark in franchise history. The team struggled at the gate, drawing more than ten thousand fans just three times in forty-one home games. The only silver lining in suffering through such a season was that the team had the third pick in the 1984 college draft. That pick would have a dramatic effect on the club's future.

Michael Jordan in a 1985 game against the New Jersey Nets. At six feet, six inches, Jordan was a significant addition to the Chicago Bulls.

Michael and the Jordannaires

On October 10, 1984, the Houston Rockets selected first in the draft and picked center Akeem (now Hakeem) Olajuwon of the University of Houston. With the second pick, the Portland Trail Blazers took center Sam Bowie of the University of Kentucky. Picking third, the Bulls got the player they wanted all along—guard Michael Jordan of the University of North Carolina.

The six-foot, six-inch Jordan had an immediate impact on the team. Chicago improved to a record of 38-44 and made it back to the playoffs for the first time since 1981. Jordan earned a starting position in the All-Star Game and won the Rookie of the Year Award.

The 1984–1985 season was also significant because of a shake-up in the front office. Shortly after the All-Star break, the league approved the sale of the Bulls to Chicago White Sox owner Jerry Reinsdorf. Reinsdorf wanted to make a complete break with the former ownership and instill new life in the organization. With this in mind, he fired general manager Rod Thorn (who had been responsible for drafting Jordan) and hired former scout Jerry Krause as the team's vice president of basketball operations. Following the playoffs, Coach Loughery (a close friend of Thorn's) was also let go. Stan Albeck was hired to coach the team for the 1985–1986 campaign.

Krause's first job was to find players to complement Jordan. He obtained forward Charles Oakley in the college draft and sharpshooting guard John Paxson from the San Antonio Spurs. The additions helped the Bulls jump out to a 2-0 start, but hope turned to despair when Jordan broke a bone in his left foot in the third game of the season. Jordan missed sixty-four games, but returned in time to help the Bulls make their way into the playoffs. Unfortunately, the Celtics eliminated Chicago in three straight games. It was obvious, however, that the Bulls were becoming a much more competitive team.

Albeck remained in charge just one year; Doug Collins replaced him as coach for the 1986–1987 season. Although Jordan led the league in scoring with an incredible 37.1 points per game, the Bulls finished at 40-42 and again were swept by Boston in the first round of the playoffs. Nevertheless, Jordan's feats brought record numbers of fans. The Bulls set a franchise attendance record by averaging 15,871 spectators per contest.

It became obvious, however, that Jordan could not win games all by himself. Krause took steps toward resolving that problem by signing Scottie Pippen and Horace Grant in the 1987 draft. The Bulls responded by winning fifty games in 1987–1988, their highest total in more than a decade. The next year, Krause obtained center Bill Cartwright from the Knicks in exchange for Oakley, and three-point specialist Craig Hodges from the Suns. The Bulls made it all the way to the Eastern Conference Finals in 1988–1989, where they lost to the eventual champions, the Detroit Pistons. With the nucleus of the team now in place, all that remained was to find a coach who could take them to the next level.

Jackson to the Rescue

Former New York Knick Phil Jackson replaced Collins as coach prior to the 1989–1990 season. The team responded positively to his calmer, more cerebral approach. Jackson put assistant coach Tex Winter in charge of the offense. Winter installed his "triangle" offense that used few set plays and instead let the players react to the way the defense was playing. After a period of adjustment to the new scheme, Chicago came on strong and finished with a 55-27 record. Jordan led the league in scoring for the fourth straight year, and both he and Pippen made the All-Star team. In the playoffs, however, the Bulls again lost to the eventual champion Pistons.

Former New York Knick Phil Jackson became coach just before the 1989–1990 season. His emphasis on defense and teamwork led the Bulls to victory.

The next year, Chicago put everything together. Jackson stressed defense and teamwork. When Jordan's amazing individual skills were added in, the combination proved to be unstoppable. The Bulls earned their second division title with a record of 61-21. In the playoffs, they were even more overpowering. Chicago swept the Knicks in three straight games, then eliminated the 76ers in five and the Pistons in four. In the finals series, the Magic Johnson–led Los Angeles Lakers won Game 1, but the Bulls bounced back to take the next four contests and win the first NBA title in the franchise's twenty-five-year history. Chicago fans finally had a championship team to call their own.

The First Dynasty

Winning an NBA title is tough enough, but repeating as champion is even harder. The Bulls, however, were up to the task. Jackson never let his squad become complacent. They won fifteen of their first seventeen games on the way to a sixty-seven-win season in 1991–1992, just two wins shy of the NBA record set by the 1972 Lakers.

The Bulls' march through the playoffs was more difficult this time. They began by sweeping three games from the Miami Heat. In the Eastern Conference Semifinals, they were extended to the limit before emerging victorious in a seven-game series against New York. The Bulls then defeated the Cleveland Cavaliers in six games to move into the finals against the Trail Blazers. The finals also went six games, with Chicago coming back from a seventeen-point deficit in the last contest to close out the series. The Bulls became only the fourth NBA franchise ever to win back-to-back championships.

If two championships in a row was difficult, three in a row was even more unlikely. Only two teams in NBA history had ever accomplished the feat: the Minneapolis Lakers (1952–1954) and the Boston Celtics (1959–1966). With B.J. Armstrong replacing John Paxson in the starting lineup, Chicago coasted to a 57-25 record in 1992–1993 for the second-best mark in the East. The Bulls swept past Atlanta and Cleveland in the playoffs, setting up an Eastern Conference Finals rematch against the Knicks.

New York took the first two games, but the Bulls bounced back to take the next four and move into the finals, where they faced the Phoenix Suns. Jordan was magnificent as Chicago defeated Phoenix in an exciting six-game series to win its third consecutive league championship. "Winning three in a row was the hardest thing I have ever done in basketball,"[9] said Jordan, who was named the NBA Finals MVP for the third year in a row. It would be his last championship for a while.

Intermission

On October 6, 1993, Michael Jordan shocked the world by announcing his retirement from basketball. He had accomplished everything there was to accomplish in the sport and needed a break from the constant media attention. Added to that was the untimely death of his father, who had been murdered that July. Jordan would go on to give professional baseball a shot while his Bulls teammates carried on without him.

They weren't quite up to the task, however, even with the addition of European standout Toni Kukoc. Chicago finished at a very respectable 55-27 and swept Cleveland in the first round of the playoffs. Their next opponent was the Knicks, who were still seething from their defeats of the previous two seasons. This time, New York got its revenge. In a thrilling seven-game series, the Knicks defeated the Bulls, ending Chicago's championship run.

The 1994–1995 season saw Chicago struggle to remain over .500 (winning more games than they lost) as Paxson and Cartwright left the team. Even playing in a new arena—the beautiful United Center—didn't help. In mid-March, the team received a big boost when Jordan announced his return to the game. He joined the club in time for the stretch run and helped the Bulls reach the playoffs. Unfortunately, after beating the Charlotte Hornets, the Bulls lost to the Orlando Magic, bringing their season to a halt. Jordan's return, however, brought Bulls' fans hope for the future.

The Second Dynasty

When the Bulls opened the 1995–1996 season, Jordan and Pippen were joined in Chicago's starting lineup by basketball's bad boy, Dennis Rodman. Under Phil Jackson's calm leadership, the threesome was awesome. The Bulls ran away from the rest of the league and finished the year with a record of 72-10, the best mark in NBA history. Work still remained to be done, however. "We've had a wonderful season," said Pippen, "but if we don't win the title, the whole season will be ruined."[10]

Pippen's fears were unfounded. In the playoffs, the Bulls swept the Miami Heat in three games, beat the Knicks in five, and swept the Magic in four to advance to the finals against the Seattle SuperSonics. The Bulls defeated Seattle in six games to bring the championship back to Chicago after a two-year hiatus.

The next year proved to be more of the same. The Bulls dominated the regular season with a 69-13 record and then raced through the playoffs. Chicago won eleven of thirteen games in dismissing Washington, Atlanta, and Miami. In the finals, they faced the Utah Jazz, who were led by Karl Malone, the league's Most Valuable Player. Utah was no match for a determined Jordan, however. The Bulls defeated the Jazz in six games for their fifth championship in seven years.

Scottie Pippen dribbles in a game against the Washington Bullets in 1997.

The Bulls repeated as champs in 1997–1998, but this time, the road to the title was not quite as smooth. Pippen missed nearly half the regular season while recovering from surgery on his left foot. The Bulls—with Jordan, Rodman, and Kukoc picking up the slack—compiled a 62-20 record in the regular season. They raced past the New Jersey Nets and Charlotte Hornets in the playoffs, but were given a scare by the Indiana Pacers, who took them to the limit before going down to defeat in the seventh game of the series. In the finals, the Bulls once again defeated the Jazz in six games, giving Phil Jackson and company their second "three-peat" of the decade, and an incredible six championships in eight years.

Rebuilding for the Future

As it is often said, all good things must come to an end. So, too, did the Bulls' amazing run of championships. Soon after the playoffs, Bulls coach Phil Jackson announced that he would not return for the 1998–1999 season. Michael Jordan followed by announcing his retirement. Former Iowa State head coach Tim Floyd was hired to replace Jackson, but the team he inherited bore little resemblance to the club that won the title. In addition to Jordan and Jackson, Pippen, Rodman, Luc Longley, Steve Kerr, and Jud Buechler all left, either through trades or free agency.

Chicago struggled through the lockout-shortened 1998–1999 season, finishing with a record of 13-37. (Disagreements over labor issues including the salary cap, free agency, rookie pay scale, and minimum salaries resulted in a 202-day lockout.) The next two years were even worse, with the Bulls compiling marks of 17-65 and 15-67, respectively. Despite their struggles, the fans continued to come out in support of their team. From 1987 through 2000, the club played before an incredible 610 consecutive sellout crowds at Chicago Center and the new United Center. "It's phenomenal," said Bulls guard Fred Hoiberg, "especially with what we've been through the past few years, for these people to still come out and support the team like they have."[11]

Unfortunately, the rebuilding process is often a slow one. As general manager Krause said, "What we're committed to doing is trying to win championships. You go through stages in the building process. The worst thing is to get to mediocrity and stay there."[12] The Bulls are showing their commitment by investing in youngsters like Ron Mercer, Ron Artest, Tyson Chandler, and Eddy Curry. It may take time getting back to the top, but Chicago fans know what it means to be patient.

Just ask those who root for the Cubs.

CHAPTER 2

Chet Walker

C het Walker was one of the early black stars of the National Basketball Association. He spent the final six years of his thirteen-year pro career with the Bulls after leaving the Philadelphia 76ers in a trade. His value to the team is illustrated by the fact that the Bulls failed to make the playoffs the year before he arrived and the year after he retired. They did qualify, however, in each of his six seasons. Walker's consistency and durability made him a valuable contributor to the Bulls during his years with the club.

Out of the Deep South

Chester "Chet" Walker was the youngest of Regenia and John Walker's ten children. He was born on February 22, 1940, in Bethlehem, Mississippi, in the middle of the Holly Springs National Forest, about forty miles south of Memphis, Tennessee. Chet grew up on a farm where, as a child, he helped his father plant and pick cotton. His mother had been a schoolteacher but had to give it up to stay home and raise her family.

Like most blacks in Mississippi in the 1940s, the Walkers were very poor. Poverty and racism in the South took their toll on

24

Chet's dad, who took out his anger and frustration on his family. He abused his wife and kids, both physically and emotionally.

When Chet was eight years old, his older sister Anna Laura contracted tuberculosis. At the time, hospitals in Mississippi were not integrated. Anna Laura had to be cared for at home, and it was there that she died in 1950 at the age of fourteen. Regenia Walker became determined that none of her other children would suffer a similar fate. Leaving her abusive husband, she and the children still living at home moved north to Benton Harbor, Michigan, where Chet's older brother, Emmett, lived.

Life in Benton Harbor was radically different for young Chet. He no longer had to use the "COLORED ONLY" bathrooms found in the South. He had his first social interaction with whites when he enrolled in the fifth grade at the predominantly white Jefferson Elementary School. It was during this time that the shy boy became interested in basketball, a sport that he could practice,

Segregated drinking fountains were commonplace in the South in the 1950s. Chet Walker left scenes such as this behind when his family moved to Michigan.

play, and enjoy by himself. As Walker later wrote in his autobiography, "I don't think there's another competitive team sport that can give you such deep satisfaction as when you dribble and shoot, just practicing by yourself. I knew very early in my love affair with basketball that this solitary play satisfied a deep part of my nature."[13]

By the time Chet began the eighth grade at Bard Junior High School in 1953, he was six feet tall and well on his way to becoming an above-average player. At Benton Harbor High School, Walker started at forward on the varsity team as a sophomore. In his very first game for coach Don Farnum's squad, Chet scored twenty points to lead the Tigers to victory. His performance made him an instant local celebrity.

Walker also played football at Benton Harbor, winning all-conference honors at tight end in both his junior and senior seasons. Basketball, however, was his sport of choice. In his junior year, Benton Harbor went to the state semifinals, where the team lost to Muskegon Heights. The next year, the Tigers made it all the way to the Class A finals in the tournament. There, they met Austin High School of Detroit. Austin was led by Dave DeBusschere, who would have many hard-fought battles with Walker over the next two decades in college and in the NBA.

Austin prevailed in the championship contest, defeating Benton Harbor, 71-68. Walker scored twenty-five points but took the loss hard. "I must have missed ten foul shots," he recalled, "and I couldn't help feeling I cost us the championship. I cried after that game . . . because the game had drawn everyone who was woven in the fabric of my life except for my mother. It was personal and local. We wanted that game for our team, our town, ourselves, and our friends and families."[14]

An All-American Career

During Walker's senior year, he was recruited by coaches from several colleges. He narrowed his choices to Bradley, Michigan, Michigan State, Western Michigan, Navy, and Nebraska. He eventually accepted a basketball scholarship from Bradley, a private university located in Peoria, Illinois.

In his first year at the school (1958–1959), Walker led the freshman team to a 15-0 record, averaging twenty-three points and sixteen rebounds a game as a six-foot, six-inch forward. The following season, he made a spectacular debut with the varsity team by scoring forty-four points against Abilene Christian in the opening game of the year. In doing so, he broke the school's single-game scoring mark. Walker quickly became a hero on campus as he led Bradley to a number four ranking in the national polls.

Later that year, the team made an extended trip through the South playing several schools in Missouri and Texas. Despite his status as a star player, Walker found himself the object of discrimination. He and the other black players were not allowed to stay at certain hotels or eat in particular restaurants. The experience was so disheartening that when the team returned to Peoria, Chet called his mother and told her he was leaving the university. Mrs. Walker was able to convince him to stay. "If you leave school, is that gonna change racism?" she asked. "It's not a perfect world. You have to find the good and enjoy it, make the most of it."[15] Walker remained at Bradley and helped lead his squad to a 24-2 record and a postseason bid to the National Invitational Tournament (NIT) at Madison Square Garden in New York City.

A Frightening Experience

Walker scored twenty-two points to lead Bradley to victory over the University of Dayton in the opening round of the tournament. The next game was the semifinals contest against St. Bonaventure. Prior to the game, Walker and teammate Al Saunders were relaxing in their hotel room when a bellhop brought up two glasses of orange juice, supposedly sent by coach Chuck Orsborn. Walker drank half of his, but Saunders decided to call the coach. Orsborn denied having sent the juice, and Walker soon began to feel ill. The police were called, but the incident was written off by most people as a prank.

Despite feeling weak, dizzy, and sick to his stomach, Walker still played that night. He somehow managed to score twenty-seven points in twenty-three minutes, leading Bradley to an 82-71 win. (Unbeknown to Walker, playing in that condition caused damage to his left kidney, a health problem that affected him from that day on.) The team followed up with an 88-72 victory over Providence in the finals to win the tournament. Still feeling the effects of the tainted juice, however, Walker scored just nine points. Although nothing was ever proved, it is likely that the doctored drink was sent by gamblers looking to affect the outcome of the game.

The NIT championship was one of the high points of Walker's college career. Bradley finished with a record of 21-5 in 1960–1961 and 21-7 in 1961–1962. Walker made first team All-America both seasons and graduated as the school's all-time leading scorer. His career statistics showed averages of 24.4 points and 12.8 rebounds per game and a field-goal percentage of .552. "Chet the Jet," as Walker was called because of his explosive moves, was clearly ready to take his game to the next level.

The Pros Beckon

Walker was selected by the Syracuse Nationals as the fourteenth overall pick in the second round of the 1962 NBA draft. His first contract called for a salary of $12,000, plus a $2,000 signing bonus. He did not have to wait long for his first play as a pro. When veteran forward Dolph Schayes was injured, Walker moved right into the starting lineup. In Walker's very first game, Elgin Baylor of the Lakers scored more than forty points against him. Walker bounced back in fine fashion, however, and averaged 12.3 points and 7.2 rebounds a game for the year. His performance earned him a spot on the league's All-Rookie team.

The next season, Syracuse owner Danny Biasone moved the team to Philadelphia, where it became the 76ers. Walker put together another fine year. His scoring average jumped to 17.3 points per contest, and he pulled down a career-high 10.3 rebounds per game. He also made the All-Star team for the first of seven times.

In January 1965, the Sixers obtained superstar Wilt Chamberlain in a trade with the San Francisco Warriors. With the Hall of Fame center added to Walker, guards Hal Greer and Wali Jones, and rookie forward Lucious Jackson, the Sixers had the nucleus of a championship contender in place. Rookie Billy Cunningham was added for the 1965–1966 season, and the team began to jell. The Sixers compiled a 55-25 record to top the East that year, but were trounced by the Boston Celtics, their archrivals, in the playoffs.

The Greatest Team Ever?

The high point of Walker's years with the 76ers was the 1966–1967 season. Philadelphia cruised through the regular sea-

Chet Walker (No. 25) on the court in a game against the New York Knicks.
Walker's high point with the 76ers was the 1966–1967 season.

son, compiling an NBA-record sixty-eight wins against only thirteen defeats. Walker averaged more than nineteen points and
eight rebounds per game as the Sixers headed into the playoffs.
There, they crushed the Cincinnati Royals, the Celtics, and the
San Francisco Warriors. In the thrilling sixth game of the finals
series against San Francisco, Philadelphia led by a single point
with four seconds left to play when Walker was fouled. He
calmly walked to the free throw line and sank both shots to
clinch the game and give the 76ers the championship. During
the playoffs, he had raised his scoring average to 21.7 points per

game for what many observers consider the greatest team in NBA history.

Walker played two more seasons with the Sixers. However, despite winning sixty-two games in 1967–1968 and fifty-five the next year, the team could not make it back to the finals. In the summer of 1969, Walker was traded to the Bulls, along with forward Shaler Hamilton, in exchange for forward Jim Washington and a player to be named later.

Walker (center) plays for the 76ers against the Boston Celtics in a 1965 game in Philadelphia.

Chet Walker celebrates with his team after winning the NBA Eastern Division Championship in 1965. The victory secured the 76ers' second straight division title.

Having spent seven years with the Sixers, Walker was taken aback by the trade. It was depressing having to leave a team that was used to being a championship contender to join one that was still in its infancy. He considered retiring rather than reporting to the Bulls, and even considered jumping to the upstart American Basketball Association (ABA). Having the ABA as an alternative helped Walker negotiate a $50,000 contract with Chicago, the highest of his career at that point. He joined the Bulls as a veteran player being asked to help take a young team to the next level.

A New Challenge

Walker joined the Bulls for the 1969–1970 season and teamed up with Bob Love to form a productive front court combination under coach Dick Motta. Walker was the player who got the ball in pressure situations. His slashing drives to the basket were sure to draw fouls from opposing players, sending him to the free throw line time and time again. He averaged 21.5 points per game and was named to the All-Star team. He also led the Bulls to a spot in the playoffs despite suffering a painful groin injury late in the season. Chicago lost to Atlanta in the postseason, but showed enough drive to give the team and its fans hope for the future.

Chester "Chet" Walker joined the Chicago Bulls for the 1969–1970 season.

The next year, Chicago won fifty-one games, twelve more than the previous season. On February 6, 1971, the Bulls faced the Cincinnati Royals in a Sunday afternoon contest at Chicago Stadium. Walker had the game of his career, scoring fifty-six points in leading the Bulls to a 119-94 victory.

Two weeks later, the Bulls met the Detroit Pistons, who led them by a half-game in the race for second place behind Milwaukee in the Midwest Division. The game was Chicago's first sellout ever, with 18,545 fans showing up to cheer their team on. The Bulls trailed by four points with forty-five seconds left in regulation time. Walker cut the margin to two with a pair of free throws, then tied the score on a jump shot after a Detroit miss. With just six seconds remaining, Walker stole the inbounds pass. After calling a timeout to set up a final play, the Bulls failed to get off a shot and the game went into overtime. In the extra period, Walker couldn't be stopped. He scored eleven of Chicago's fourteen points, giving him a total of forty-four for the night. The Bulls edged the Pistons, 115-114, and Chicago held on in second place the rest of the season.

Over the next four seasons, Walker was a model of consistency. He averaged between nineteen and twenty-two points per game each year, teaming up with Bob Love to form a lethal one-two scoring combination. Chicago kept coming up short in the playoffs, however, losing in the Western Conference Semifinals in 1971–1972 and 1972–1973, and in the Conference Finals the next two seasons.

After six solid years with the Bulls, Walker asked the club for a $200,000 salary for 1975. The Bulls' management did not want to invest that much money in a thirty-five-year-old forward, and refused to trade or release him. With his options severely limited, Walker went to court and sued the Bulls and the league for federal antitrust violations. He lost the case and decided to retire rather than sign at a lower salary. "Physically I started to wear down," he explained. "Mentally it was difficult to constantly get up for every game."[16] The move proved to be costly for the Bulls. The next season, they won only twenty-four games and failed to qualify for the playoffs.

On to Hollywood

During his years in the NBA, Walker had become friends with Zev Braun, a Beverly Hills producer. Looking for new worlds to conquer, Walker moved to California to try his hand at the movies as an independent film producer. Success was not instantaneous, as he later recounted in a 1985 interview for *HOOP* magazine. "The adjustment was very difficult,"[17] he said.

One of Walker's first successes as a producer was *Freedom Road*, a 1980 NBC miniseries. He followed that with 1983's *The Fiendish Plot of Fu Manchu*, Peter Sellers's final movie. His greatest producing triumph thus far has been *A Mother's Courage: The Mary Thomas Story*. The made-for-television movie tells the story of Mary Thomas, the mother of former NBA star Isiah Thomas, and

Detroit Pistons guard Isiah Thomas waves from a jet. Walker coproduced a film about Thomas's mother, Mary Thomas, and her struggle to raise nine children.

her struggle to raise nine children as a single parent in an inner-city neighborhood. The movie had a special meaning for Walker. "I saw Isiah's struggle growing up on the West Side of Chicago," he said. "The story of Isiah's mother is so similar to my own life."[18] Walker received numerous accolades as coproducer of the 1989 film, including an Emmy Award, television's highest honor. He continues to produce films today.

Walker is leaving his mark on the movies just as he did on the basketball court. In thirteen NBA seasons, he scored nearly nine-teen thousand points, compiling identical averages of 18.2 points per game in both the regular season and the playoffs. Walker was extremely durable, and retired as one of just a handful of players to have appeared in over one thousand games. He played an important role on one of the greatest teams in history, and was an important factor in establishing the Chicago Bulls as an NBA franchise.

CHAPTER 3

Bob Love

B ob Love was a quiet superstar, appreciated by his teammates and coaches but often overlooked by the everyday fan. He overcame one adversity after another to become a three-time All-Star, and led his team in scoring six times. Love was the Bulls' all-time leading scorer until being surpassed by Michael Jordan. Together with Chet Walker, Love formed one of the most productive forward combinations in league history.

A Poor Beginning

Robert Earl Love was born in Delhi, Louisiana, on December 8, 1942. His mother, Lula Bell Hunter, was only fifteen years old when he was born. His father, Benjamin Edward Love, was in the army, having recently been drafted. Robert's parents had never married, so he was born on the plantation where his mother and grandparents worked and lived. When his grandmother refused to let Lula Bell go back to work after the boy's birth, the plantation owner made the family leave. William Hunter, Robert's grandfather, packed their belongings into a rickety old mule-driven wagon. The sixteen members of the clan—Robert, Lula Bell, her parents, and her twelve brothers and sisters—piled in and traveled to nearby Tallulah, where they stayed for a year. The Hunters eventually settled in Bastrop, where Robert lived until he went away to college.

Robert's mother eventually married a man named Lee Cleveland. Baba, as he was called, seemed to resent the youngster. When Baba was younger, he and Robert's natural father had been rivals for Lula Bell's affections. Robert was a constant reminder of his mother's affair with Benjamin Love.

By the time Robert was four years old, he had started stuttering. His fear of his stepfather added to his problem since Baba often beat the boy for any little reason. Robert found himself spending more and more time at his grandparents' house, where Ella Mae and William treated him like a son. Although the Hunter house lacked many modern conveniences such as electricity and indoor plumbing, Robert felt very comfortable there. "There was always a feeling of joy and warmth about that house,"[19] he later recalled.

Robert Earl Love, better known as Bob Love, on the court for the Chicago Bulls.

Robert began attending Our Lady of Help Christian School as a first grader. He had problems, however, right from the start. The nuns at the school believed in strict discipline and had no experience in dealing with his problem. He was often slapped on the hands for his stuttering. After three months, his mother took him out and enrolled him at Morehouse Parish Training School. The teachers there made attempts to help him, but without much success. Robert was teased by the other kids, and by the third grade, his stuttering had gotten worse.

Around that same time, Baba's abuse became unbearable. Robert eventually moved in with his grandparents. He would stay with them until he went away to college.

Emergence of an Athlete

The teasing that Robert was subjected to caused him to withdraw further into himself. His shyness intensified in junior high school when his stepbrother died and his favorite aunt left school after getting pregnant. He couldn't understand why everything seemed to be happening to him. His grandmother helped him through this difficult time. "Robert Earl," she said, "wasn't but one perfect person walked this earth. Everybody got a handicap or disability. . . . You gotta have a dream and you got to keep it. You got to hold on to your dream. No matter how bad things may look."[20] He never forgot this advice.

Robert was very athletic and soon found that his talent for sports helped him gain acceptance from others. He turned all his attention toward sports, particularly basketball and football. Since his family could not afford to buy him a backboard and basket, he formed a wire coat hanger into the shape of a hoop and nailed it to the side of his grandparents' house. Then he took one of his grandfather's socks and filled it with paper and grass. He shot baskets with the homemade ball for hours on end.

Robert made his high school football team as second-string quarterback in the ninth grade. The next year, he started and led Morehouse to the state championship. The team repeated its success in his junior year, and fell one point shy of winning a third consecutive championship when he was a senior.

Despite his success in football, Robert was drawn more and more to basketball. He tried out for Morehouse's powerful varsity team as a junior and made the squad as a reserve. At forward he averaged eight points and five rebounds a game as the team duplicated the football squad's success and won the state championship.

Over the summer, Robert worked hard to hone his basketball skills. In his senior year, he was the star of the team, averaging twenty-eight points a game. Although Morehouse lost in the second round of the state tournament, the six-foot, six-inch Love was chosen for the All-State team at forward. (He also made All-State in football.)

Even though he excelled as an athlete, Love still lacked confidence in himself as a person. It took his high school music teacher, Mrs. Delarose DuBose, to make him start believing in himself. One day, during a discussion of classical music, Mrs. DuBose shocked her class by saying, "We have a great artist right here in our class. . . . Robert Love is a very unusual person. He is gifted. On the basketball court, he's as smooth and flawless as the men we've been talking about. He is an artist."[21] From that day on, Robert was determined to show everyone that she was right.

College and the Pros

After Love's stellar senior year, colleges began to show an interest in him. He accepted a scholarship from Southern University, an all-black school located in Scotlandsville, Louisiana, just outside of Baton Rouge. He began classes there in the fall of 1961. Surprisingly, college proved to be less stressful on Love than high school. Classes required less participation and, therefore, fewer opportunities for embarrassment. For the most part, he had little difficulty with college work. He eventually graduated with a degree in food and nutrition.

In sports, Love decided to concentrate solely on basketball. He made the varsity team as a freshman and averaged thirteen points per game for coach Richard Mack. In each succeeding year, his totals went up, reaching a high of thirty-one points per game in his senior season. He also improved his rebounding with averages of ten, fifteen, and eighteen per game over his final three years. Love made the National Association of Intercollegiate Athletics (NAIA) All-America team in each of those seasons.

At the end of his senior year (1965), Love was invited to try out for the U.S. national basketball team. He made the final cut and traveled around the country as the U.S. club played the Russian team in a seven-game series. After playing four years at a small all-black college, it was his first real national exposure. Love impressed the pro scouts who saw him play, and he was selected in the fourth round of the 1965 NBA college draft by the Cincinnati Royals. Together with his new wife, Betty, whom he had married in his senior year at Southern, Love traveled to Cincinnati for the team's rookie camp.

With the NBA consisting of only nine teams at the time, competition for spots on the roster was fierce. Even though Love played well during the exhibition season, the Royals did not have

Love showed great promise during his college years, and made the National Association of Intercollegiate Athletics All-America team three seasons in a row.

room for him on opening day. They asked him to play a season with the Trenton Colonials of the Eastern League in order to get some experience. Love had a great year for the Colonials, averaging twenty-two points and fifteen rebounds per contest. By the next year, he was ready for the NBA.

The Road to Chicago

Love was one of the twelve players on the Royals' opening day roster for the 1966–1967 season. His teammates included all-time greats Oscar Robertson and Jerry Lucas. Robertson took the youngster under his wing and taught him the subtleties of the game, such as catching the ball with knees bent so as to be in position to shoot quickly.

Love did not play much as a rookie. His year was cut short when he injured his back and had to be operated on for a herniated disk. He finished the season averaging just six points a game, but earned a reputation as a solid defensive player. The next year proved to be more of the same.

In the summer of 1968, the NBA held an expansion draft to help stock the Milwaukee Bucks and Phoenix Suns, two new teams that had recently been admitted into the league. Love was drafted by the Bucks and led the team in scoring during the exhibition season. Shortly after the season began, however, he was told by Milwaukee general manager John Erickson that he was being cut. One of the reasons he was given was his inability to communicate well because of his stutter.

Rather than being cut, however, Love was instead sent to the Bulls—together with guard Bobby Weiss—in a trade for Flynn Robinson. Love suffered an injury in an automobile accident that kept him on the injured reserve list at the start of the season. When he returned to action, his role was that of defensive specialist, just as it had been in Cincinnati. He averaged just under six points a game for the year, and began to wonder if he would ever get the opportunity to show what he could do as a starter.

A Star Is Born

The Bulls made some changes for the 1969–1970 season, but Love again began the year on the bench. When forward Bob Kauffman was hurt, coach Dick Motta moved Love into the starting lineup. He responded by averaging twenty-one points a game, leading the team in scoring for the first of seven consecutive seasons. With an offense built around Love, forward Chet Walker, and guard Norm Van Lier, the Bulls improved their record by six games and earned a spot in the playoffs. Although they were beaten by the Atlanta Hawks, the future looked bright.

The next year, Love averaged over twenty-five points a game and set a franchise record with 2,043 points scored and 3,482 minutes played. He was named to the All-Star team for the first time and won All-NBA Second Team and All-Defensive Second Team honors. The Bulls began to come together as a team and won fifty games for the first time in the club's history.

Love blossomed into one of the league's top players. In addition to his steady defense, he could be counted on to score at least 20 points per game. He reached a high of 25.8 points in 1971–1972, finishing sixth in the league in scoring for the second year in a row. The next year, he scored 49 points in back-to-back games against the Bucks and the Kings (formerly the Royals). His

23.1 points per game average helped him earn his third and final All-Star Game appearance.

With Love and Walker leading the way, the Bulls were serious contenders throughout the first half of the 1970s. They never made it to the NBA Finals, however, falling in the postseason to the Lakers in 1971, 1972, and 1973; the Bucks in 1974 (after having beaten the Pistons for the team's first playoff series victory ever); and the Warriors in 1975. Failing to win a championship ring was Love's biggest regret as a pro.

Bulls guard Norm Van Lier on the court in a 1974 game against the Milwaukee Bucks. Van Lier was often teamed with Bob Love and Chet Walker for a winning offensive combination.

Love is presented with the game ball in Chicago for scoring his 10,000th point in a game against the Seattle SuperSonics. Love could be counted on to score at least 20 points per game.

Considering his accomplishments, Love never received the attention accorded many of the league's other stars. As *Chicago Tribune* columnist Robert Markus wrote in 1975, "Love has been the Bulls' top scorer ever since he began to play regularly. He is also the team's top defensive forward and one of the best in the league. There are few two-way performers in the NBA in a class with Love. Yet he is probably the least-publicized player on his own team."[22]

The main reason for this lack of recognition was Love's stuttering problem and difficulty communicating. "I used to dream I was Martin Luther King or JFK," he said, recalling the pain. "I'd pretend I was a great speaker like them standing before an audience of thousands of people, and the words would flow out like music."[23] Unfortunately, this was only a dream. Journalists would walk right past Love in the locker room after games to speak with players they could count on for comments or quotes. Love used this slight as a motivational device. He wanted to show everyone that he was as good as, if not better than, his other more-publicized colleagues. More often than not, he succeeded.

The End of the Line

The Bulls won the Midwest Division title in 1974–1975 and faced Golden State for the Western Conference crown. Love had again led the team in scoring during the regular season with an average of twenty-two points per game. He raised that to twenty-three for the playoffs, but the Bulls fell to the Warriors in an exciting seven-game series.

The following year, Chicago got off slowly as a rift developed between Coach Motta and several of the players. Chet Walker had announced his retirement, and both Love and Norm Van Lier became embroiled in contract disputes. Morale was down to an all-time low, and it was reflected in the team's play. Chicago finished the year with a record of just twenty-four wins and fifty-eight losses, the worst record in the league. Coach Motta resigned after the season and Ed Badger took his place.

Following the 1975–1976 season, the American Basketball Association disbanded and four of its teams were absorbed by the NBA. Shortly after the next season got under way, Love was traded to the New York Nets, one of the former ABA clubs. He was not at full strength physically as his back and knees were causing him a great deal of pain. Seeing that he was not performing up to his former level, the Nets dropped him a month into the season. Love played out the rest of the year with the Seattle SuperSonics and averaged just seven points a game. By that time, it was obvious his back problem was more serious than originally thought. Sadly, he was forced to retire from the game he loved.

Putting His Life in Order

Life after basketball was not easy for Love. He went on many job interviews but kept coming up empty. He finally realized the seriousness of his speech impediment. His inability to communicate well was preventing him from being hired for positions for which he was otherwise qualified. Despite having his college degree, he was forced to take jobs digging ditches, washing dishes, and delivering food. Added to this were marital problems that eventually ended with his wife filing for divorce in 1983.

Love married another woman, named Denise Bouldin, and shortly afterward had surgery on his back. He was told he would probably have to walk with a cane for the rest of his life. Denise eventually walked out on him, leaving a note that read, "I didn't want to be married to a guy who couldn't speak and I definitely don't want to be married to a guy who's going to be a cripple for the rest of his life."[24]

With his life seemingly spinning out of control, Love was hired to wash dishes and bus tables in the cafeteria of Nordstrom's department store in Seattle. "Oh, it was so embarrassing," he later recalled in an interview for the *Sporting Life*. "People would come in and recognize me and whisper stuff about me being an all-star, now lookit him. It was awful."[25]

It did not take long for Nordstrom's management to appreciate that Love was a hard worker. He was approached by John Nordstrom, one of the store's owners, who said, "We think you could have a future with our company, and we'd like to help you get your life together. But first, you'll have to do something about your speech. If you're willing to give it a try, we'll pay for it."[26]

Love jumped at the opportunity. He began seeing a woman named Susan Hamilton from the Seattle Speech and Hearing Clinic. At age forty-five, with her help, he was finally beating the handicap that had dogged him all his life.

As part of his therapy, Love began giving motivational speeches before different groups. At one of these speeches, an executive from the Chicago Bulls happened to be in the crowd. Soon after, Love was contacted by the team and offered a job as director of community relations. He gratefully accepted and has remained with the club in that capacity since 1992. Since then, Love's life has taken a turn for the better. In January 1994, his uniform became the second one to be retired by the team (Jerry Sloan's was the first). In December of the following year, he married Rachel Dixson during a half-time ceremony at a Bulls-Spurs game.

Bob Love is living proof that with hard work and a will to succeed, a person can overcome a handicap and make his or her dream come true. Love blended his talent for scoring together with above-average rebounding and defensive skills to become one of the premier forwards of his day. This would not have been possible without his belief in himself and his abilities. As he wrote in his autobiography, "If you play the victim, you will always be one. If you want to succeed, you have to move on and go for your dream."[27]

CHAPTER 4

Michael Jordan

To many people who follow basketball, Michael Jordan is the greatest player ever to lace up a pair of sneakers. "When God decided to create the perfect basketball player and send him down here," said broadcaster and former NBA player Fred Carter, "He gave him to the Jordans."[28] Jordan combines a deadly shooting touch, strong rebounding, deft passing, and smothering defense in a package not found in any other player in league history. In addition to having been the heart and soul of the Bulls, Jordan is a role model for an entire generation and an ambassador for the game wherever he goes.

The Genesis of Greatness

Michael Jeffrey Jordan was the fourth of James and Deloris Jordan's five children. He was born on February 17, 1963, in Brooklyn, New York, where his father was undergoing training as a mechanic. Shortly after Michael's birth, the family moved to the town of Wallace, North Carolina. They eventually settled in Wilmington when Michael was seven years old. James worked at the General Electric plant while Deloris got a job in a bank.

Although the family sometimes had to struggle to make ends meet, the children never lacked for love. Early on, Michael's parents taught the boy right from wrong, and stressed the importance of hard work. "We try to make something happen," said James in a 1984 interview, "rather than waiting around for it to happen."[29]

As a youngster, Michael's favorite sport, in which he excelled, was baseball. In 1975, the Dixie Youth Baseball Association named him Mr. Baseball among North Carolina twelve-year-olds. Michael's father encouraged his sons in all sports and built a backyard court where the boys could play basketball every day. Whenever James was hard at work on such a project, he had a habit of sticking his tongue out. Michael imitated his father, and the habit became one of his signature mannerisms when he played ball.

According to his family and friends, Michael's fierce competitiveness came about as a result of his intense rivalry with his older brother, Larry. Although shorter than Michael, Larry was an outstanding player. The competition between the siblings brought out the best in each other and helped generate a lasting love and respect for one another. "Larry always used to beat me on the backyard court," recalled Michael. "His vertical jump is higher than mine. He's got the dunks . . . and most all the same stuff I got. And he's 5-feet 7-inches! Larry is my inspiration."[30]

At Laney High School, Michael was a pitcher and centerfielder on the baseball team. He tried out for the varsity basketball team as a five-foot, nine-inch sophomore, but did not make the squad. "It was embarrassing not making that team," he remembered. "They posted the roster and it was there for a long, long time without my name on it. I remember being really mad, too, because there was a guy who made it that really wasn't as good as me."[31]

Rather than sulk, Michael used the snub as motivation to improve his game. And improve it he did. He averaged twenty-five points per contest for the junior varsity team and then made the varsity squad, where he averaged twenty points a game as a junior. That summer, he attended the prestigious Five Star Basketball Camp in Pittsburgh and made quite an impression. Michael went on to average twenty-three points per game as a six-foot, six-inch senior at Laney, and was named to the McDonald's High

*Michael Jordan is considered a role model for an entire generation and an
ambassador for the sport of basketball.*

School All-America team. He received numerous scholarship offers and finally accepted one from the University of North Carolina (UNC), where he played for legendary coach Dean Smith.

From the Tar Heels to the Bulls

Jordan started for North Carolina from his first game as a freshman in the 1981–1982 season. Playing on the same squad as All-
Americans James Worthy and Sam Perkins, he showed flashes of
brilliance as he averaged 13.5 points and four rebounds a game.
He blended well into Coach Smith's system, which emphasized
team play rather than the talents of any one individual player.
The Tar Heels finished the season as the nation's number-one
ranked team with a record of twenty-four wins against only two
losses.

Jordan plays in a 1984 game for the University of North Carolina Tar Heels, his college team.

North Carolina was one of the favorites to win the National Collegiate Athletic Association (NCAA) tournament that spring. Led by Worthy and Perkins, the Tar Heels made it to the finals, where they faced mighty Georgetown University and seven-foot freshman sensation, Patrick Ewing. The two teams battled back and forth for thirty-nine minutes. With thirty-one seconds left in the game, Georgetown held a one-point lead. After calling a time-out, North Carolina tried to get the ball to either Worthy or Perkins for the final shot. Both players were covered, however, and the ball swung around to the freshman Jordan. He launched a sixteen-foot jump shot that went in to give UNC a 63–62 victory and Coach Smith his first national championship. It was a dramatic ending to a memorable freshman year for Jordan, and gave him a place in college basketball lore. As UNC assistant coach Eddie Fogler said,

"The kid doesn't even realize it yet, but he's part of history now. People will remember that shot 25 years from now."[32]

Jordan followed up his freshman year by being named the *Sporting News* College Player of the Year in his sophomore season. "He soars through the air," gushed the paper, "he rebounds, he scores, he guards two men at once, he vacuums up loose balls, he blocks shots, he makes steals. Most important, he makes late plays that win games. Call it what you may, court sense or court presence, he has it."[33] Jordan averaged 20 points per game that year in a well-balanced UNC attack. He averaged 19.6 points per game as a junior, and again won Player of the Year honors. With nothing more to prove in the college ranks, Jordan declared himself eligible for the 1984 NBA draft. It was a decision for which the Chicago Bulls would forever be thankful.

"Love of the Game"

The 1983–1984 Bulls were one of the NBA's worst teams. They finished the season with a record of 27-55, drawing an average of just 6,365 fans per game. Because of their poor record, they had the third overall pick in the college draft. With that pick, they selected Jordan, who signed a seven-year $6 million contract.

At the time, the NBA's Uniform Player's Contract included a clause that prevented a player from taking part in certain activities during the off-season—including playing basketball—in order to protect the team's investment. Jordan knew he couldn't live with that kind of restriction. He became the first player to negotiate what he called a "love of the game clause" that allowed him to play basketball any time he wanted.

With the contract out of the way, Jordan was anxious to prove he was worth every penny he stood to receive. Before he had a chance to do so, however, he joined the U.S. team that was to represent the country in the 1984 Los Angeles Summer Olympics. The squad played a series of exhibition games against a team of NBA All-Stars to get them ready for the competition. The plan worked to perfection. With Jordan leading the way, the U.S. squad raced past China, Canada, Uruguay, and Spain to take the Olympic gold medal. In a touching moment at the award ceremonies, Jordan took his gold medal and placed it around his mother's neck.

Individual Brilliance

Jordan made his pro debut with the Bulls on October 26, 1984. He scored 16 points in that first effort against the Washington Bullets, with his play giving hints as to what was to come. He proceeded to win NBA Rookie of the Year honors, averaging 28.2 points, 6.5 rebounds, and 5.9 assists per game. Unusual for a rookie, he also starred on defense, averaging more than two steals a contest.

Even more impressive than his numbers, however, was the way he played the game and the excitement he brought to Chicago Stadium. He soared through the air, dunking the ball and performing athletic, gravity-defying moves never before seen. Jordan hated to lose, and drove himself to give 100 percent at all times.

Jordan on the court against the Boston Celtics. Although the Bulls lost, Jordan set an NBA playoff record by scoring 63 points in a single game.

Jordan's value to the Bulls was demonstrated the next year. He suffered a career-threatening foot injury that kept him out of action for all but eighteen games. Against his doctor's recommendations, he returned to action near the end of the season. Jordan helped the Bulls make the playoffs, where they faced the mighty Boston Celtics. In Game 2 of the series, he put on a magnificent show, scoring a playoff-record sixty-three points in Chicago's 135-131 double-overtime loss.

Jordan led the league in scoring for the first time in the 1986–1987 season. He scored 50 points against the Knicks on opening night and proceeded to average 37.1 points per game for the year. Fans came out to see Jordan in record numbers, but the team remained mediocre, finishing at 40-42.

The next year, Jordan was even more magnificent. He averaged thirty-five points per game to win his second scoring title and also led the league in steals.

Jordan's popularity soared as he averaged 37.1 points per game during the 1986–1987 season.

During the All-Star Weekend, he won the slam-dunk championship for the second consecutive year and then won Most Valuable Player (MVP) honors in the game by scoring forty points to lead the East to a 138-133 victory. He capped his season by being named the league's MVP and its Defensive Player of the Year. Despite all his individual success, however, the Bulls could not get past the Pistons in the Eastern Conference Semifinals of the playoffs.

NBA Champs

The Bulls added center Bill Cartwright for the 1988–1989 season and finished the year with a record of 47-35. The opening round of the playoffs found Chicago matched up with the Cleveland

Cavaliers. With the series tied at two games apiece, Cleveland led the final game by one point with time running out. Jordan got the ball and made a remarkable shot for the winning basket despite being guarded closely by Cleveland's Craig Ehlo. Jordan went up for his shot with Ehlo's hand in front of the ball. He hung in the air—seemingly defying gravity—until Ehlo began to come down. He then shot the ball, and made the basket. "The Shot," as it came to be known, put the Bulls into the second round of the playoffs. There, they defeated the Knicks before going on to lose to the eventual champions, the Detroit Pistons.

Although Jordan again led the league in scoring in 1989–1990 (including a career-high sixty-nine points in a game against the Cavaliers), the Bulls again fell short of a title. The next year, however, they would not be denied. Chicago compiled a franchise-best record of 61-21, then raced through the playoffs to their first NBA crown. The victory was the culmination of years of hard work for Jordan. "When I came here," he said, "we started from scratch. I vowed we'd make the playoffs every year, and each year we got closer. I always had faith I'd get this ring one day."[34]

In the summer after the Bulls' first championship, Jordan received criticism from some people following the publication of *The Jordan Rules*. The book by *Chicago Tribune* writer Sam Smith detailed problems between Jordan and other members of the team. The Bulls did not let the mini-controversy, however, interfere with their quest for a second title. After Chicago defeated the Portland Trail Blazers to win the crown, Jordan said, "This season was unbelievable for me and for us as a team. We went through a lot of adversity. . . . Last year was more for the city and the organization and the fans. This year, it's a little more selfish. This one is for my teammates and me."[35]

Almost immediately after the end of the season, Jordan began practicing with what became known as the Dream Team. The Dream Team was a squad of NBA All-Stars who would represent the United States in the 1992 Summer Olympic Games in Barcelona, Spain. The team steamrolled over the competition, and Jordan earned the second gold medal of his career. This was followed by the Bulls' third consecutive championship crown, a feat accomplished by only two other teams in NBA history. As Jordan explained afterward, "It's something for a team to win three in a row in this era, when there is so much talent in the league and so much parity."[36] It was also something that all-time greats such as Larry Bird, Magic Johnson, and Isiah Thomas never did. Jordan seemed to have few fields left to conquer.

A Break from the Game

That summer, Michael Jordan's seemingly perfect life was shattered by a personal tragedy. His father, James, was brutally murdered in his car on a lonely road in North Carolina. Michael was devastated. He had always been especially close to his father, who had been one of the guiding forces in his life. "When James Jordan was murdered," he said, "I lost my dad. I also lost my best friend."[37] Making the tragedy even harder to accept were wild rumors that hinted that the killing was somehow connected to gambling losses that Michael had incurred. (In fact, the murder was the result of a random robbery attempt.)

The devastating loss seemed to rob Jordan of some of his desire to continue playing ball. That October, he shocked the entire basketball world by announcing his retirement from the game at age thirty. "I've always stressed to the people who know me," he explained, "that when I lose my sense of motivation as a basketball player, then it's time for me to move away from the game. . . . I've reached the pinnacle of my career and I don't feel like I have anything left to prove."[38]

It was not long, however, before Jordan found a new challenge. He signed a contract with the Chicago White Sox, the baseball team owned by Bulls' owner Jerry Reinsdorf. Jordan joined the minor league Birmingham Barons to fulfill his childhood

Michael Jordan rounds the bases during his brief stint with the Chicago White Sox.

dream of playing professional baseball. His skills on the baseball diamond, however, did not match his skills on the hardwood. After batting just .202 in the 1994 season, his chances for making the major leagues seemed dim. Rumors began to surface that he might return to the NBA.

The Comeback

The Bulls' record was 34-31 when Jordan returned to action in March 1995. In just his fifth game back, after being out for nearly eighteen months, he scored fifty-five points and led Chicago to a win over the New York Knicks. The Bulls won thirteen of seventeen games after Jordan's return to make their way into the playoffs. In the postseason, however, Shaquille O'Neal and the Orlando Magic proved to be too much for them to handle. The Bulls were eliminated by Orlando in six games.

Late in the 1995 season, briefly wearing jersey No. 45, Jordan helped the Bulls win thirteen of seventeen games, which landed them in the playoffs.

Over the summer, Jordan worked hard to get himself into the best possible shape, determined to prove he could once again lead the Bulls to a championship. With the 1995 addition of Dennis Rodman, the Bulls added a rebounding component to the team that it desperately needed. The club got off to a fast start and never looked back. The Bulls won forty-one of their first forty-four games and ran away with the Central Division title. They finished with seventy-two wins for the season, setting a new NBA record. Jordan won his eighth scoring title and was named the league's Most Valuable Player for the fourth time. The Bulls went on to win another crown and claimed their place among the greatest teams in league annals. "The historians will decide our

After defeating the Utah Jazz 90-86 in the 1997 NBA finals, Michael Jordan shows off the championship trophy.

place among the greatest teams," said Jordan. "I'm happy I'm back and I'm happy to bring a championship back to Chicago."[39]

But Jordan wasn't done yet. The Bulls won again in 1997, defeating the Utah Jazz in the finals. The victory was especially satisfying since Jazz forward Karl Malone had been named the league's MVP for the regular season. Jordan completely outplayed him in the playoffs, including a miraculous thirty-eight-point effort in Game 5 while suffering from the stomach flu. "I almost played myself into passing out," he later recalled. "I was almost dehydrated. I couldn't breathe."[40]

The next year, it appeared that Chicago's run at the top might finally come to an end. Rumors surfaced that the team might not bring back Phil Jackson as coach and that they might try to trade Scottie Pippen. Jordan felt the club could win another championship if Jackson and Pippen were brought back, and he made his feelings known to management. With his contract up, he threatened to leave if the nucleus of the team was broken up.

Jordan and Jackson eventually signed one-year contracts, and Pippen was retained. With Jordan winning his tenth scoring title and fifth MVP Award, the Bulls won sixty-two games to tie for the best record in the league. In the playoffs, Jordan led Chicago to its third consecutive title, and sixth in eight years, averaging better than thirty-two points per game. Jordan became the NBA's all-time leading scorer for the playoffs. He capped off the year by winning his sixth NBA Finals MVP Award. As broadcaster and former NBA star Isiah Thomas put it, "Michael Jordan has taken basketball to heights we never thought it would go."[41] For the Bulls, it meant one final taste of glory.

Retirement Once and for All?

On Wednesday, November 13, 1999, Michael Jordan appeared at a news conference at the United Center to announce his retirement from professional basketball. He had ended his career in storybook fashion by making the game-winning shot with just 5.2 seconds to go in the last game of the finals series against Utah. "There's a way to go out as an athlete," said teammate B.J. Armstrong, "and that's the way to go out."[42]

At the news conference, Jordan explained the reason for his decision. "Mentally," he said, "I'm exhausted. I don't feel I have a challenge."[43] When pressed, he said he was "99.9 percent" certain he would never return. With an income from endorsements estimated at $45 million per year, he said he would enjoy life with his family, doing the things he never had a chance to do before. (Those endorsements included deals with Nike, McDonald's, Sara Lee, General Mills, and Quaker Oats. According to *Forbes* magazine, Jordan was responsible for adding $10 billion into the U.S. economy.)

The opportunity to do one of those things presented itself a short time later. On January 19, 2000, Jordan became the president of basketball operations and part owner of the Washington Wizards. The job presented him with a new challenge: to help build and develop a team from the management side of the game.

As much as Jordan enjoyed his new position, he still missed being out on the court. So, it was not a complete shock when he announced to the world in September 2001 that he would play basketball once again, this time for the Wizards. When a reporter asked why he was coming back, his reply was short and sweet. "For the love of the game," said Jordan, "nothing else."[44]

The Legacy

Jordan has had a significant effect off the court as well as on it. He established the Jordan Family Institute at the University of North Carolina and helped build the James R. Jordan Boys and Girls Club and Family Life Center in memory of his father. In addition, he is a member of the board of America's Promise and is involved in the United Negro College Fund, the Make-a-Wish Foundation, and the Special Olympics. Jordan's business ventures include a line of athletic shoes and apparel for Nike and involvement in several restaurants. He also starred in the movie *Space Jam* and has hosted the *Saturday Night Live* television show.

Jordan's position as one of the most outstanding athletes of the modern day is supported by his list of achievements on the basketball court. Entering the 2001–2002 season, he stands first in NBA history in scoring average, third in steals, fourth in points, fifth in field goals made, sixth in field goals attempted, and seventh in free throws made and attempted. He also holds both the NBA Playoffs and All-Star Game career record for highest scoring average. His other records and awards could fill an entire book.

His effect on the game of basketball, however, cannot be measured by mere numbers. Jordan plays with a flair and exuberance rarely seen. His athletic ability and aerial maneuvers have drawn gasps of amazement from fans around the globe. He has helped solidify the game's standing on the international stage and become the most celebrated athlete of the modern day, and arguably of all time. In an age when the term "superstar" is applied to even the most ordinary of players, Michael Jordan may be the only one to whom it does not do justice.

CHAPTER 5

Scottie Pippen

S cottie Pippen may well be the second-best all-around player to
grace NBA courts over the past decade, with shooting, rebounding, passing, and defensive skills rarely found in one player.
Unfortunately, he may not have received the acclaim he deserves
since, for most of that time, he was a teammate of the league's top
player, Michael Jordan. Pippen's all-around skills were not unap-
preciated by his more famous teammate. "I know he makes me a
better player," said Jordan. "Unfortunately, it may take a while, after we both retire, for people to realize just how good Scottie Pippen really was." [45]

Early Struggles

Maurice Scotty Pippen was born on September 25, 1965, in the
rural town of Hamburg, Arkansas. (He later changed the "y" in
"Scotty" to "ie.") He was the youngest of twelve children born to
Ethel and Preston Pippen. Preston worked long, hard hours at the
Georgia-Pacific paper mill to support his large family until suffer-
ing a stroke when Scottie was in the ninth grade. The stroke left
Preston confined to a wheelchair, unable to speak.

Although the family did not have many of life's luxuries, there
was never a shortage of playmates to help them occupy their

time. As a youngster, Scottie's favorite sports were baseball and football. When he was introduced to basketball at age eleven, he fell in love with the game. He practiced with his friends and family for hours on end, but his size kept him from becoming an immediate star. At Hamburg High School, he made the team as a six-foot-tall sophomore, but played infrequently. When prospects for his junior year did not look much better, Scottie skipped the team's preseason conditioning program in order to serve as manager for the football team. Coach Donald Wayne was furious and wanted to cut him from the basketball squad, but he changed his mind when Scottie's teammates begged him to reconsider. As a reserve, however, Pippen again saw little action.

Scottie Pippen catches a pass from Michael Jordan during a 1991 NBA game. Pippen brings his shooting, rebounding, passing, and defensive skills to each game.

Scottie dramatically improved all aspects of his game in the summer following his junior year. As a senior, he became the team's starting point guard. As Wayne remembered, Pippen was "nothing tremendous, but good. Not flashy, but consistent."[46] At six-foot-one and 150 pounds, however, he drew little interest from college recruiters. Coach Wayne intervened on his behalf and called his old friend Don Dyer, who was the head coach at the University of Central Arkansas (UCA). He convinced Dyer that, although Scottie might not be good enough to make the team, he had experience as a team manager and could help out as a practice player. Pippen joined UCA in that capacity in the fall of 1983. It did not take Dyer long to realize that his student manager was actually the best player on the team.

Pippen became a Chicago Bull in 1987, and averaged 7.9 points and 3.8 rebounds a contest his rookie season.

Pippen made the varsity team as a six-foot, three-inch freshman and was starting by midseason. He blossomed as a sophomore, recording 18.5 points and 9.2 rebounds per game from the point guard position. By this time, Dyer was aware of Pippen's potential. "I remember thinking at the end of his sophomore season that Scottie had a chance," he recalled. "I'd seen Sidney Moncrief and Darrell Walker play . . . at the same stage, and they both made it [to the NBA], and I thought Scottie was bigger and better."[47]

Pippen continued to grow, and by his senior year, he stood six-feet, seven-inches tall. Because of his previous experience, he was still able to handle the ball like a much smaller man. "The surprising thing to me," said former UCA assistant basketball coach Arch Jones, "is that he never lost any of his coordination in all of this growing. He was able to take the skills he had learned when he was smaller and use them when he was bigger."[48] In his senior year, Pippen averaged 23.6 points, 10 rebounds, and 4.3 assists a game and was selected as an NAIA All-American.

Attracting the Pros

Because Central Arkansas was such a small school, few people saw Pippen play. One who did was NBA talent scout Marty Blake. Blake advised teams to take a look at the young man, but only Jerry Krause of the Bulls followed up on his suggestion. Krause was impressed by the reports he received on Pippen and intended to select him in the 1987 draft. Before he had a chance to do so, however, Blake invited Pippen to a postseason all-star event in Portsmouth, Virginia. There, he impressed all the scouts in attendance and was named to the all-tournament team. He followed this up with an equally impressive performance in another tournament in Hawaii, and the secret was out.

Knowing Pippen would likely be taken before the Bulls had a chance to draft him, Krause arranged a deal with the Seattle SuperSonics. Seattle agreed to take Pippen with the fifth pick, then send him to Chicago in exchange for center Olden Polynice, whom the Bulls would choose eighth, and a future draft choice. The deal was announced during the draft, and Pippen became a Bull.

Pippen missed part of preseason practice because of contract negotiations between the rookie's agent, Jimmy Sexton, and the team. He finally agreed to a six-year contract calling for more than $5 million. Pippen reported to the squad and became the backup at small forward behind Brad Sellers.

Playing about twenty-one minutes per game, Pippen averaged 7.9 points and 3.8 rebounds a contest in his rookie season. He gave some indication of his potential by recording ninety-one steals, ranking second on the team. He handled the ball well for a man his size, possessed extraordinary quickness, and was an intimidating defender. The Bulls improved their record by ten games over the previous season, and finished second in the Central Division.

In the fifth and deciding game of Chicago's first-round playoff series against Cleveland, Pippen made his first start as a pro. He responded by scoring twenty-four points, grabbing six rebounds, and making three steals in the Bulls' 107-101 victory. His performance was all the more remarkable because he was slowed by a late-season back injury. The injury would require surgery in the off-season, causing him to miss part of training camp for the second year in a row.

Pippen claimed the small forward spot in the starting lineup in December 1988, shortly after returning to action. He raised his scoring average to over fourteen points per game as the Bulls again made their way into the playoffs. After defeating the Cavaliers and Knicks, Chicago faced Detroit in the conference finals. In the first minute of the deciding sixth game, Pippen was elbowed in the head by Detroit's Bill Laimbeer. Suffering the effects of a concussion, Pippen did not return to action. "He is a tougher kid than most people think," reported Krause. "He begged me to let him go back into that game. . . . But, in the end, I had to go with the doctor's advice."[49] The Bulls lost to the Pistons, coming up short in their quest for a championship.

All-Star Status

Pippen came into his own as a player in the 1989–1990 season. New Bulls coach Phil Jackson took advantage of his all-around skills by designating him the team's "point forward," a combination of point guard and small forward. Pippen welcomed his new responsibilities. "I felt it was time for me to do what I should have been doing a long time ago," he said, "to blossom as the complete player that I always felt I could be."[50] Pippen started every game for the Bulls and averaged 16.5 points per contest. He also finished third in the league in steals. For his performance, he was named to the NBA All-Star Game for the first time.

The Bulls again faced the Pistons in the Eastern Conference Finals, hoping to avenge their loss of the previous season. Such was not to be the case, however. The series went to a seventh game in which Detroit beat Chicago to again end their dreams of a championship. During the pregame warmups, Pippen had been stricken by a painful migraine headache. He played forty-two minutes despite pain he later likened to having an ice pick lodged in his skull. Obviously affected, he made just one of ten field-goal attempts in the Bulls' 93-74 loss.

Although Pippen's father had died earlier in the playoffs, he refused to use that as an excuse for his below-average performance. Instead, the death had a calming effect on him. As he later told Sam Smith in an interview for the Chicago Tribune, "the things that have happened . . . to me, have helped me grow up.

Especially the passing of my father. That was something that took me to another level of growing and maturing. That's when I started to be more of a man."[51]

Pippen's maturation was one of the key forces that drove the Bulls in the 1990–1991 season. Pippen had received an unfair amount of blame in the media for the Bulls' defeat in the final

Despite coping with his father's death and struggling with severe migraine headaches, Pippen matured as a player during the 1989–1990 season.

game of the playoffs and was determined to have a big season. "I thought about it all summer," he said. "I failed to produce."[52]

One thing he did was consult with a doctor about his migraines. The doctor suggested eyestrain as a possible cause and proposed that he wear glasses when he wasn't playing ball. Pippen took his advice and the headaches stopped.

Although Pippen was no longer distracted by migraines, the Bulls lost their first three games of the season, but quickly got on track. Pippen was installed as the team's primary ball handler and responded by leading the club in assists. He finished second on the team in scoring and steals behind Jordan and second in rebounding behind Horace Grant. Pippen had improved so much, many observers now considered him the second-best all-around player in the league, behind teammate Jordan.

Chicago compiled a 61-21 record during the regular season and won the first division championship in the franchise's history. In the Eastern Conference Finals, the team faced the Pistons for the third straight year. This time, the results were different. The Bulls swept Detroit in four straight games to move into the NBA Finals against the Los Angeles Lakers, who were led by superstar guard Magic Johnson.

Michael Jordan was his usual magnificent self during the finals, but Pippen was just as important to the Chicago cause. After the Lakers won the first game, Pippen sparked the team to a win in Game 2 by holding Johnson to just fourteen points in a stalwart defensive effort. He scored twenty points himself as the Bulls tied the series at one game apiece. With the momentum having changed, Chicago proceeded to win the next three games to clinch their first NBA championship.

All-Around Brilliance

The Bulls repeated as champions in 1991–1992 as Pippen averaged over twenty points per game for the first time in his pro career. He also set new highs in rebounds and assists and was named to the NBA's All-Defensive team for the first time. Chicago could no longer be considered a one-man team, and Pippen was rightly proud of his contribution. "Michael [Jordan] is a great player," he said, "but he wasn't MVP of the league until we played together. All of the success we had was because we did it together."[53]

That summer, another honor came Pippen's way. Along with Jordan, he was selected as a member of the U.S. Olympic Dream Team that would represent the country in the 1992 Barcelona Games. The squad, featuring the game's greatest stars, was one of the most talented teams ever put together. The team fulfilled all expectations, dominating play and returning home with the gold medal. Pippen enhanced his growing reputation with an outstanding performance in international competition.

With almost no time off to relax, Pippen returned to the NBA. He again teamed with Jordan to lead the Bulls to a third consecutive championship. The fans recognized his talents by making him the second-leading vote-getter in the All-Star balloting, behind only his illustrious teammate. It would only be a matter of time, however, before he would step out from behind that enormous shadow.

A Season of Ups and Downs

In the summer of 1993, Michael Jordan shocked the basketball world by announcing his retirement. The mantle of leadership on the team was passed to Pippen. Many observers predicted rough times for the club, but after a slow start, the Bulls came on strong and were 34-13 at the All-Star break. In the midseason classic, Pippen had his brightest moment. He was the dominant player on the court, scoring twenty-nine points, pulling down eleven rebounds, and making four steals to defeat the East to a 127-118 victory. For his efforts, he was the unanimous selection as the game's Most Valuable Player.

Pippen maintained his all-around excellent play during the second half of the season and helped lead the Bulls to a record of 55-27. His 22 points, 5.6 assists, and 2.93 steals per game were all team-high marks, and he was named to both the All-NBA and All-Defensive first teams.

Unfortunately, the loss of Jordan was too much for the Bulls to overcome during the playoffs. They swept the Cavaliers in the first round and faced the Knicks in the conference semifinals. The series marked perhaps the darkest moment of Pippen's pro career.

The Knicks won the first two games in New York, and the series moved on to Chicago. In Game 3, the Bulls trailed by a point with just 1.8 seconds left to play. After time-out was called, Coach Jackson set up a play in which Toni Kukoc was to take the final shot. Kukoc was a former Croatian star who had been signed to a large contract by the Bulls prior to the start of the season. Pippen thought the play should have been designed for him and made perhaps the biggest mistake of his career. In a shocking move, he refused to reenter the game for the final seconds. He remained on the bench as Kukoc sank the game-winning basket.

From 1995 to 1998, Pippen remained remarkably consistent, averaging 19.7 points and 6.2 rebounds per game.

Jackson was able to defuse the situation, but Pippen's reputation was tarnished. He was accused of being selfish and letting his team down. To his credit, he owned up to his mistake and accepted the blame. "I really apologize for that," he would later say. "I am human. I'm allowed to make mistakes, and [it's] something I've put behind me right now. I've asked the fans to forgive me for that, and hopefully I can go on with my life."[54]

The Bulls bounced back to tie the series at two games apiece, but in Game 5, Pippen was frustrated once again. With Chicago leading by one point with time running out, he was called for a foul on New York's Hubert Davis. NBA Supervisor of Officials Darrell Garretson later admitted it was a bad call, but Davis nonetheless made the two free throws to give the Knicks an 87–86 win. Although the Bulls came back to win Game 6, New York won the final game to end the Bulls' run of three consecutive championships.

Three More Rings

The 1994–1995 season was one of discontent for Pippen. In order to guarantee his future, he had signed a five-year, $18 million extension to his contract in June 1991. By 1994 standards, however, he was underpaid, ranking fifth on the Bulls in salary. He felt he deserved more and became frustrated. To his credit, he did not allow his frustration to affect his play. Despite rumors of a possible trade, he became only the second player in league history to lead his team in every major statistical category.

Michael Jordan returned toward the end of the season, but the Bulls were defeated by the Orlando Magic in the playoffs. With Jordan and Pippen again teaming up, however, prospects for the future were bright. The pair formed an unstoppable duo and led the Bulls to three more championships over the next three years. Pippen remained remarkably consistent. Over the three-year period, he averaged 19.7 points, 6.2 rebounds, 5.8 assists, and 1.8 steals per game.

Pippen's slam dunk contributed to the Bulls' 104-102 victory over the New York Knicks in the 1994 NBA Playoffs.

Winning six titles in eight years was a remarkable achievement. "It's something that I'll be able to look back and cherish for the rest of my life," said Pippen. "It's been a lot of fun, and that's part of winning—being able to have the courage and desire to go out and do whatever you can to bring your team to the top."[55] Unfortunately, the Bulls' time at the top was coming to an end.

In a 1998 game against the Seattle SuperSonics, Pippen lunges for the ball.
He was traded to the Houston Rockets the following year.

Good-Bye, Chicago

Following the 1997–1998 season, Michael Jordan retired for the
second time and Phil Jackson announced he would not return as
coach. The Bulls' management decided it was time for a new beginning. On January 22, 1999, Chicago traded Pippen to the
Houston Rockets in exchange for Roy Rogers and a second-
round draft pick.

Houston hoped Pippen could team with veterans Hakeem
Olajuwon and Charles Barkley to bring the team an NBA cham-

pionship. Unfortunately, that did not happen. Pippen averaged 14.5 points per game and led Houston in assists, but he never seemed comfortable in the team's half-court offense. The club was eliminated by the Lakers in the first round of the playoffs. That October, Pippen was on the move again. This time, he was traded to the Portland Trail Blazers for six players.

As a member of the Trail Blazers, Pippen has reached several career milestones. He recorded his two-thousandth steal, five-thousandth assist, and seventeen-thousandth point in 2000, and played in his one-thousandth NBA game the following year. He has not, however, been able to bring the NBA title to Portland.

Pippen has achieved status as one of the 50 Greatest Players in NBA History.

As he faces the twilight years of his pro career, Pippen has much to be proud of. He has been named to the All-NBA first team three times and the NBA All-Defensive first team seven times. He has made seven appearances in the All-Star Game, six times as a starter. He has won six championship rings and two Olympic gold medals (in 1992 and 1996). In 1996, Pippen received perhaps his greatest honor of all. The skinny kid from the tiny University of Central Arkansas was selected as one of the 50 Greatest Players in NBA History.

CHAPTER 6

Phil Jackson

Phil Jackson was good enough to last thirteen seasons in the NBA as a role player, someone who has one particular talent, such as rebounding or defensive skills. The time he spent on the bench was not wasted, for he observed and analyzed New York Knick coach Red Holzman's every move. By the time Jackson got his chance to coach the Bulls, he had developed a distinctive coaching style all his own. His use of Tex Winter's triangle offense, coupled with his own unusual motivational techniques, helped make him the most successful coach of his era. During the 1990s, he guided the Bulls to six championships.

A Nomadic Childhood

Philip Douglas Jackson was the youngest of Charles and Elisabeth Jackson's four children. He was born in Deer Lodge, Montana, on September 17, 1945. Charles was a Methodist minister who met his future wife when they both joined the Assemblies of God religious movement. According to Sam Smith of the *Chicago Tribune*, Elisabeth was a "brilliant and prophetic evangelist who was credited with performing miracles."[56]

Because of the couple's work, the family moved from town to town every couple of years. Phil did not have much stability in

During the 1990s, coach Phil Jackson led the Bulls to six championships using techniques he learned from watching other great coaches.

his life until they eventually settled in Williston, North Dakota, where Charles was appointed a regional superintendent of churches.

Phil inherited his athleticism and competitiveness from his mother, who had been a star basketball player. He participated in every sport he could, including baseball, football, hockey, and track and field. Phil had been introduced to basketball while in the fifth grade in Great Falls, Montana. By the time he entered the seventh grade, it had become his favorite sport.

At Williston High School, Jackson made the varsity basketball team as a six-foot, one-inch sophomore, but saw little action. By observing coach Bob Pederson, however, he quickly learned the nuances of the game. "As the season progressed," he said, "I began to recognize the logic behind every cut, every screen, every defensive adjustment. Before long, I was able to anticipate the immediate possibilities and make advantageous moves or countermoves. My vision and my timing were a step ahead of the other players, so I could react to situations before the defense was ready."[57]

By his senior season, Phil had grown to six-feet, six-inches and 180 pounds. He led Williston to the state tournament, where the Coyotes faced Grand Fork Central in the finals. Jackson scored a career-high forty points to lead Williston to victory in the first state championship game ever televised throughout North Dakota.

Evolution of a Basketball Philosophy

The exposure Jackson received increased his standing as a prospect in the eyes of college coaches. He received seventy scholarship offers from around the country, but chose to stay close to home and play basketball at the University of North Dakota. There, he came under the influence of coach Bill Fitch, whose disciplined approach to the game stressed fundamentals and defense. "The way I played and the attitude I brought to basketball," says Jackson, "was developed a lot by Fitch."[58]

Jackson majored in philosophy, psychology, and religion, and intended to follow his father into the ministry when he graduated. On the basketball court, he became a two-time Division II All-American whose forty-two-inch arm length helped make him a demon on defense. His hustle, desire, and enthusiasm made up for what he lacked in the more refined basketball skills such as shooting, rebounding, and passing. (They were also the basis of his nickname, "The Mop," given because of his penchant for diving after loose balls.) In Jackson's three varsity seasons, his scoring average jumped from 11.8 to 21.8 to 27.4. His average rebounds per game also increased each year, from 11.6 to 12.9 to 14.4.

Jackson caught the eye of New York Knicks coach Red Holzman, and the team selected him in the second round of the 1967 college draft. Jackson, however, did not intend to play professionally. "I'm very pleased the Knicks thought so highly to draft me," he told Holzman, "but I'm having second thoughts. My original plans were to attend graduate school and become a minister. I still think about that." [59] Holzman was persuasive, however, and he convinced the gangly young man to give the pro game a chance. Jackson did so and quickly became a disciple of his coach's team-oriented style of play.

Although Jackson originally planned to attend graduate school and become a minister, he joined the New York Knicks in 1967.

NBA Champions

The Knicks of the late 1960s were building a powerful team. They were led by Willis Reed, Walt Frazier, Bill Bradley, and Dave DeBusschere. Unable to break into the starting lineup, Jackson's role was to spark the team coming off the bench, providing a surge of energy when the starters were beginning to show signs of tiring. He became a favorite of the fans with his aggressive, emotional style of play. In his rookie year of 1967–1968, he averaged 6.2 points and 4.5 rebounds per game. Although the numbers were not especially impressive, they were good enough to earn him a spot on the NBA All-Rookie team.

After raising his scoring and rebounding averages slightly in his second year, Jackson suffered a severe back injury that forced him to miss the entire 1969–1970 season. He closely watched Holzman's moves as the coach guided the team to an NBA championship. He returned to action the

Jackson makes a layup in a 1974 NBA game. During this year he scored an average 11.1 points per game, the highest of his career.

next year and helped the club to another title in 1972–1973. The following year, he scored a career-high 11.1 points per game.

After eleven years with the Knicks, Jackson was traded to the New Jersey Nets on June 8, 1978. There he served two years as a player and assistant coach. After thirteen NBA seasons, he finished with a career average of 6.7 points and 4.3 rebounds per game as a valuable sixth man off the bench. Jackson led the NBA only one time during his career. Symbolic of his aggressive play, his 330 personal fouls in 1974–1975 topped the league.

Following his time with the Nets, Jackson spent a year as a color commentator on the team's television broadcasts. His heart, however, was in coaching. Unfortunately, during his playing days, he had gained a reputation as a free spirit. He became known as the "flower child of the New York Knicks"[60] because of his unconventional lifestyle. Jackson sported a beard, blue jeans, and wire-rimmed glasses, and gave the appearance of being a hippie. In his 1975 autobiography, *Maverick*, he admitted to having smoked marijuana and having experimented with drugs. "I didn't do hard drugs," he said. "I had done a couple of LSD trips, but I wasn't a user, abuser, or a person that's addicted—I'm not an addictive person—but I am a person that likes to try a variety of experiences."[61] Partly because of his reputation, teams were afraid to hire him and he was forced to go to the Continental Basketball Association (CBA) to gain experience.

In 1982, Jackson was hired as head coach of the CBA's Albany Patroons. He guided the team to the league championship in 1984. The next season, he was named the circuit's coach of the year. In spite of his success, Jackson was not able to develop a team the way he wanted. The CBA acted as a kind of minor league for the NBA. Players got a chance to develop their skills, but as soon as they reached a certain level of proficiency, NBA teams would sign them to fill open spots on their rosters. Because of this, there was little continuity with CBA clubs. "I like to see how a team evolves," explained Jackson, "and in the CBA it was a revolving door. The league's purposes really weren't meant for the kind of coaching I wanted to do."[62]

A Return to the NBA

After five seasons at the helm of the Patroons, Jackson felt he had nothing more to prove. He left the team and began looking for another position. He missed out on a chance at becoming the head coach at Yale University and considered entering law school.

Finally, in the summer of 1987, he was contacted by Bulls general manager Jerry Krause. Krause offered him a job as assistant coach under Doug Collins. "What I saw in Phil was an innate brightness," explained Krause, "a feel for people . . . a probing

Coach Jackson gives courtside advice to Michael Jordan. Jackson became coach of the Chicago Bulls on July 10, 1989.

mind."[63] Jackson remained in the position for two years. When the Bulls failed to live up to management's expectations, Collins was fired. On July 10, 1989, Jackson signed a four-year contract as the team's new head coach.

Chicago management appreciated the fact that Jackson had played under Red Holzman's team-oriented system. "[Holzman] believed primarily in defense," said Jackson at his first press conference, "that you let the offense dictate itself. . . . And that's my belief. Hit the open man, see the ball and get back on defense. You'll see a team using speed and quickness in an up-tempo game."[64]

One of Jackson's first jobs was to convince Bulls superstar Michael Jordan to accept his role in the new triangle offense designed by assistant coach Tex Winter. The triangle stressed ball movement and spread the offensive burden among all five players on the court. It was a big change for Jordan, who often controlled the flow of the game all by himself. Jackson convinced Jordan that the system would force the defense to guard all the players and thus take some defensive pressure away from him. After some initial skepticism, Jordan agreed to give it a try, with the understanding that he could still take over at the end of the fourth quarter if the outcome of a game was undecided.

Jackson's plan was a success in its very first year. After struggling early on, the Bulls came on strong to finish the season with a record of 55-27, second behind the defending NBA champion Detroit Pistons in the Central Division. After beating Milwaukee and Philadelphia in the playoffs, the Bulls were finally stopped by the Pistons in an exciting seven-game series. The last game, an embarrassing 93-74 loss, was what Jackson would later call "my most difficult moment as a coach."[65] The Bulls had come up short, but it was obvious that they were a team on the rise.

The Dynasty

With Scottie Pippen developing into one of the best players in the league, Chicago won sixty-one games the next year to wrest the Central Division crown away from Detroit. The Bulls defeated the Knicks by forty-one points in the first game of the playoffs, and proceeded to run roughshod over New York, Philadelphia, and Detroit to reach the NBA Finals. The Lakers won the series opener, but the Bulls bounced back and took the next four games to win the first championship in the franchise's history. The clincher in Los Angeles was especially sweet for Jackson. "For me it was doubly special," he recalled, "because the Forum was where I had won the championship as a player nearly 20 years earlier."[66] With the win, Jackson also earned a place in trivia history as the first coach to win championships in both the NBA and CBA.

Chicago repeated its success the next season, compiling a 67-15 mark in the regular season. Jackson kept the team focused on basketball despite the publication of a book that depicted Jordan as selfish and temperamental. Later in the year, charges that Jordan lost large sums of money on golf bets also provided a distraction. Under Jackson's guidance, however, the club raced through the playoffs and defeated Portland for its second consecutive championship.

Jackson rallied the Bulls to a third straight title in 1992–1993, a feat that just three teams in league history had accomplished. Playing Phoenix for the title, the Bulls became the first team to win the first two games of an NBA Final on the road. In Game 7,

An enthusiastic leader, Jackson by 1997 had guided the Bulls to six championships in eight years.

John Paxson's three-point basket with 3.9 seconds remaining proved to be the clincher. Jackson would label the championship "Three the Hard Way."

In 1993–1994, Jackson did perhaps his finest job of coaching. Despite losing Jordan—arguably the greatest player in the history of the game—to retirement, Jackson coached the Bulls to fifty-five victories. But Chicago lost to the Knicks in the playoffs, with one game being decided on a foul on Scottie Pippen.

Jordan returned to action toward the end of the 1994–1995 season, but the Bulls fell to Orlando in the playoffs. The next year, however, the team regained its magic. In addition to having Jordan for the entire season, the Bulls added Dennis Rodman, the league's best rebounder. With Jackson giving the team direction, Chicago went on to set an NBA record with a 72-10 mark in the regular season. The Bulls proceeded to win fifteen of eighteen playoff games, giving them their fourth championship of the decade.

In 1996–1997, the Bulls started their "Drive for Five" by winning seventeen of their first eighteen contests. They breezed through the regular season and then defeated the Utah Jazz for the crown. It appeared that their run at the top might be over, however, as rumors flew that Jackson might not be re-signed and Pippen might be traded. When Jordan threatened to retire if the nucleus was broken up, Chicago management scrapped its plans and signed Jackson to a one-year contract. With Jordan winning his fifth Most Valuable Player Award, Jackson guided the Bulls to an incredible sixth championship in eight years. The team had cemented its standing as one of the greatest teams in NBA history.

A New Direction

Despite the club's extraordinary success, things were not all well with the Bulls. With Michael Jordan considering retirement, management decided the club's reign at the top was at an end. Scottie Pippen was traded, and Dennis Rodman and several other players were allowed to leave as free agents.

During the season, tensions had grown between Jackson and the front office. Krause had alienated his coach by trying to claim most of the credit for the Bulls' success. "It's a ball club's management that wins championships,"[67] said Krause, in effect belittling Jackson's contributions. It was one of the factors that entered into

Jackson's decision to step down from his job. As he later explained, "There's no doubt that the particular stress of this past season, and of my entire nine years coaching in Chicago, has affected me in many ways. . . . I've . . . been worn down by the frequent disputes with management, by the constant traveling, the game preparation, the players, and the high-level energy of game-time sights and sounds that were piped through my system over a hundred times every year."[68]

Jackson left Chicago with a record of 545 wins and only 193 losses in his nine seasons as head coach. He spent the next year as an adviser for the presidential campaign of Senator—and former Knick teammate—Bill Bradley. Basketball was never far from his mind, however, and when the Los Angeles Lakers came calling, Jackson signed a five-year contract, calling for $6 million per season, to become the team's coach beginning with the 1999–2000 season.

Although the Lakers had two of the game's greatest players in Shaquille O'Neal and Kobe Bryant, they had not won a championship since 1988. That would all soon change. Using unorthodox methods that included giving players selected books to read, hiring a specialist to give them breathing lessons, and encouraging them to use yoga and meditation, Jackson led the team to the NBA title in his first season at the helm. "He's a man who feels a lot of peace and calm and that transfers to the team," said forward A.C. Green. "When guys out on the floor start to get crazy, he settles things down. He just doesn't seem to get rattled."[69]

Jackson continued to perform his magic in 2000–2001. Despite an ongoing feud between O'Neal and Bryant, he again guided the Lakers into the playoffs. There, they dominated play as no other team had done before. They breezed through the postseason, losing just one game to win their second consecutive NBA crown.

Despite his amazing success, Jackson still has his detractors. Many point out that each of his championship teams has included arguably the two best players in the game—Michael Jordan and Scottie Pippen in Chicago, O'Neal and Bryant in Los Angeles. They overlook the fact that Jordan and O'Neal played a combined thirteen NBA seasons without winning a single title before Jackson became their coach.

Whether or not Jackson is one of the greatest coaches of all time is open to debate. What cannot be denied, however, is that he is one of the most successful. His eight championships as a coach are second to Red Auerbach's nine on the all-time list. He stands second to only Pat Riley in most NBA playoff victories, and his playoff winning percentage is by far the highest in league history. By the time he is ready to retire, his record will likely be his ticket to the Basketball Hall of Fame.

CHAPTER 7

Dennis Rodman

W ithout question, Dennis Rodman is literally the most color-ful personality in the history of the National Basketball As-sociation. His multihued hair, tattoos, and body piercings took away from the fact that he was arguably the greatest rebounding forward the league has ever seen. In a time when scorers get all the attention, Rodman was an exception who took greater pride in his defensive, rather than offensive, skills. He was an integral part of the Bulls' championship teams of the 1990s.

In Need of Direction

Dennis Keith Rodman was born in Trenton, New Jersey, on May 31, 1961. His father, Philander Rodman, was an air force man sta-tioned in New Jersey. He left his wife, Shirley, when Dennis was three years old. Shirley took the boy and his two sisters, Debra and Kim, and moved to her native Dallas, Texas.

The family struggled to make ends meet while living in the Oak Cliff housing project. "I had never worked a day in my life," said Shirley, "but I wanted to support [my children], to give them a life without depending on welfare."[70] She took whatever jobs she could to put food on the table for her family. Unfortunately, the time she spent at work was time away from her children. Dennis was quiet and shy. He made few friends and kept mostly to himself. He was active in sports but was not as athletic as his two sisters. Both girls starred on their high school basketball team.

Dennis tried out for the South Oak Cliff High School football squad as a sophomore but was cut. At a rail-thin five foot, six

Dennis Rodman grabs a rebound during the 1996 playoffs against the Miami Heat. He was an integral part of the Bulls' championship teams of the 1990s.

inches, the youngster simply was too small. He did make the junior varsity basketball team, but quit in the middle of the season because of a lack of playing time.

Dennis graduated from high school but had no plans for the future. He had taken a maintenance job at the Dallas–Fort Worth Airport in order to earn some money. His sisters, meanwhile, both received basketball scholarships to schools where they would achieve All-American status (Debra to Louisiana Tech and Kim to Stephen F. Austin).

Hitting Bottom

While working late one night, Rodman made a bad mistake. He stole sixteen watches from an airport shop and gave them away to his family and friends. The nineteen-year-old did not realize that he had been captured in the act by airport security cameras. Soon afterward, he was arrested and taken to jail. He was kept in a cell overnight and learned a hard lesson. Rodman prayed to God and promised his mother he would change his ways. He helped the police recover the stolen items, and in return, the charges against him were dropped.

Rodman managed to stay out of trouble, but his life still lacked direction. He continued to be lazy and unmotivated and cared only about hanging out with his friends. Then came the lucky break that changed the course of his life: Over a period of a little more than one year, he grew eleven inches. The skinny five-foot, nine-inch high school youngster now stood a gawky six feet, eight inches. "Just like that," he remembered. "It was like I woke up one day and had a new body."[71]

Rodman's growth spurt enabled him to become a dominating basketball player at the recreation center where he played. A family friend recommended him to Bill Broom, the assistant basketball coach at Cooke County Junior College in Gainesville, Texas. Broom was impressed enough with Rodman to offer him a full two-year scholarship. Rodman quickly accepted and proceeded to average 17.6 points and 13.3 rebounds a game in his first season. His coaches appreciated his dedication on the court. "He would do the dirty work," said Broom, "he'd play defense, and he would put in the hours. . . . And because of that, he really developed quick."[72]

Unfortunately, Rodman did not apply that same work ethic toward his studies. He lost his scholarship, flunked out of school, and returned home. His mother had had enough. When Rodman refused to return to school or get a regular job, she kicked him out of the house. "She was always strong," said Rodman of his mother. "Her best move was to kick me out of the house at an age when all I wanted to do was bum around. She told me, 'The hell with that,' and I got her message."[73]

After six months of living on the streets, Rodman begged his mother to let him return home. She agreed, on the condition that he meet with Lonn Reisman, an assistant basketball coach at Southeastern Oklahoma State University, a small NAIA school located in Durant, Oklahoma. Reisman had seen Rodman play at Cooke County and was interested in recruiting him. "He didn't apply himself when he got his first opportunity," said Shirley. "In my mind, this was his last chance."[74]

Reisman talked Rodman into visiting the school's campus with him. Once there, he told Rodman he thought he had a chance for a future in professional basketball. Rodman signed a letter of intent, determined to make the most of this new opportunity.

A Lasting Friendship

Reisman and head coach Jack Hedden got Rodman a summer job at Southeastern's annual basketball camp for youngsters. While there, Rodman befriended Bryne Rich, a troubled young boy from nearby Bokchito. Bryne had been in a deep depression for some time since the death of his best friend in a hunting accident.

With basketball as a common interest, the twenty-two-year-old black counselor and the twelve-year-old white boy grew close. Rodman helped bring Bryne out of his depression, and the two became inseparable. At the end of the summer, Rodman was invited to the Riches' ranch, where he lived for three weeks as a member of the family. Bryne's father became the father figure that had been missing from Rodman's life.

All-American

When Rodman began the fall semester at Southeastern, he quickly established himself as the star of the basketball team. Bryne accompanied him to many of the team's games and eventually became the squad's water boy. Rodman helped lead the

Savages to an 18-9 record and a spot in the conference playoffs. While averaging 26.1 points and 12.6 rebounds a game, he was named a First Team NAIA All-American and the Oklahoma Intercollegiate Conference Player of the Year.

The following year (1984–1985), Rodman followed up with another All-American season. He helped his team reach the NAIA Tournament for the first time in more than twenty years. It was there that he first came to the attention of NBA scouts. Their interest in him grew during his senior year when he led the NAIA in rebounding and averaged 24.4 points per game. For his accomplishments, Rodman earned All-American honors for the third consecutive year.

In the summer of 1986, Rodman's wildest dream became a reality. As he sat in the Riches' living room watching the NBA draft on television, he heard his name called. He had been selected in the second round, with the twenty-seventh overall pick, by the Detroit Pistons. "It was a happy day," said Pat Rich, Bryne's mother. "But in ways, it was kind of sad. We knew he was heading off into a new life."[75]

As a member of the Detroit Pistons, Rodman was named Defensive Player of the Year two seasons in a row.

The Bad Boys

That fall, Rodman joined a veteran Pistons squad coached by Chuck Daly. The rookie played sparingly in his first season, averaging just fifteen minutes a game. By carefully observing other players, however, he came to an important conclusion. He decided that his best chance at having a long, successful pro career would be to specialize in one aspect of play. Since rebounding had been one of his strengths in college, he decided he would channel his energies in that direction in the pros.

Coach Daly was delighted by Rodman's fanatical devotion to rebounding and defense. Despite averaging a career-high 11.6 points per game in his second year, Rodman's aggressiveness on the boards, or rebounds, was the part of his game that most impressed his coach. By the 1988–1989 season, Rodman was an important cog in Detroit's rotation. In addition to concentrating on defense, he also shot well enough that year to lead the league in field-goal percentage with a mark of .595. For his efforts, he finished as the runner-up for the NBA Sixth Man Award, given to the best reserve player in the league.

The Pistons became known for their physical style of play, a style that gave rise to the team's nickname, the Bad Boys. Although their manner of play was considered dirty by some, it was successful. The Pistons won the NBA championship in both 1989 and 1990. In the latter year, Rodman—by now a starter— was selected for his first All-Star Game and was named the NBA Defensive Player of the Year.

The next year, Rodman again won Defensive Player of the Year honors as he led the NBA in offensive rebounds. However, it was only a hint of what was to come. In 1991–1992, he led the league in total rebounding, averaging a remarkable 18.7 boards per game, the highest mark in the league in twenty years.

Although he led the league again the following season, Rodman's off-court behavior began to be erratic. Coach Daly, who had become a fatherlike figure to him, had resigned at the end of the 1992 season. Rodman was also going through a hard time in his personal life. He was going through a divorce and was depressed over being separated from his daughter. He began a pattern of being late to practices and games. To those around him, it was obvious he wanted out of Detroit.

Dennis the Outrageous

Rodman received his wish prior to the 1993–1994 season when he was traded to the San Antonio Spurs. By this point in his career, he had achieved a good measure of success and fame. He had been garnering a lot of publicity for what many considered his rebellious behavior on and off the court. (In addition to his fines and suspensions for coming late to—and missing—practices and meetings, he had also begun having slogans and messages shaved into his hair.) Rodman enjoyed his notoriety and decided he would al-

Rodman's brightly colored hair, tattoos, and body piercings quickly garnered him media attention both on and off the court.

ways express himself as an individual with his own identity, no matter what anyone else might think. One way in which he expressed this individuality was by dyeing his hair various bright colors. In explaining his new style, he said, "I'm going to be me. . . . I like to show the wildness, the puzzle that is Dennis Rodman."[76]

Rodman quickly became a media sensation. His hair, tattoos, and body piercings made him the most visible player in the league. On the court, he received numerous technical fouls and ejections for rough play, including a $5,000 fine for head butting John Stockton of the Utah Jazz. NBA commissioner David Stern called Rodman in for a meeting to discuss his penchant for getting into trouble, but it did not have much effect. The Spurs put up with his antics as they continued to win games.

Eventually, however, Rodman wore out his welcome. He and head coach Bob Hill were constantly at odds, with Rodman refusing to follow directions. A dispute over a contract extension caused a rift with the front office, adding to the tensions. Despite winning two more rebounding titles in his two seasons with the Spurs, Rodman was traded to the Chicago Bulls on October 2, 1995.

Rodman was traded to the Bulls in 1995. He played for them in this 1996 game against the Miami Heat.

Three More Rings

Many NBA observers were amazed that the Bulls would take a chance on the high-risk Rodman. Their need for a rebounder, however, made the risk worthwhile. Chicago gambled on its belief that Michael Jordan and coach Phil Jackson would be able to keep Rodman in line. A wild lifestyle and gambling losses had caused Rodman to fritter away most of the money he had earned with the Pistons and Spurs. He needed to produce in order to maintain the lifestyle to which he had become accustomed. "We made an agreement that he would come here with a clean slate," said Jackson. "We were going to ignore what had gone on before; whatever problems he had in the past would stay in the past."[77]

The gamble worked out to the benefit of both parties as Rodman bought into Jackson's philosophy. "My approach is to just allow Dennis to be the best professional he can be," said Jackson, "and to make him understand that any behavior that interferes with his on-court performance is unacceptable."[78] Rodman's rebounding was just what the Bulls needed to bring Chicago another NBA title. The club won a league-record seventy-two games in the regular season and then steamrolled through the playoffs. Rodman won his fifth consecutive rebounding title and joined Jordan and Scottie Pippen on the league's All-Defensive first team. And during the playoffs, he twice tied Elvin Hayes' NBA Finals record of eleven offensive rebounds in a single contest.

Rodman became the darling of Chicago's basketball fans. They loved his colorful personality, the energy he brought to the game, and his blue-collar work ethic. They even forgave him for an ugly incident in March in which he was suspended eight games for head butting a referee in a game against the New Jersey Nets. For once, he seemed sorry for his actions. "I felt like I had let the team and the fans down," said Rodman. "The Bulls were treating me good, and so was the whole city of Chicago, and then along comes something like this."[79]

Unfortunately, Rodman's unruly behavior began to be more of a distraction to the team. In December 1996, he was suspended from two games for making derogatory comments about NBA commissioner David Stern and the league referees. An even uglier incident made headlines a month later when he kicked a photographer he had tripped over while going after a loose ball. For this transgression he was suspended eleven games, the second-longest such punishment in league annals.

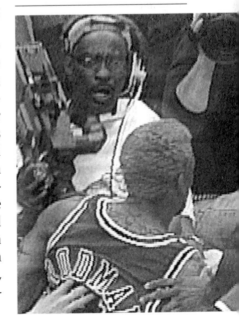

Cameraman Eugene Amos looks at Dennis Rodman in disbelief after Rodman kicked him in the groin during a game against the Minnesota Timberwolves in 1997.

Rodman's defiant attitude extended into the postseason. At one point, he was assessed at least one technical foul in thirteen consecutive playoff games. During the finals against the Utah Jazz, he capped his season by making a disparaging remark about Mormons. Although he tried to apologize, the league still assessed him a record $50,000 fine.

The Bulls won the NBA title again that season, and garnered a third consecutive crown in 1997–1998. Rodman won three rebounding championships in his three years with the team. That summer, however, the team was dismantled. Jordan and Jackson announced they would not be back, and Pippen was traded to the Houston Rockets. Rodman also left as the Bulls' remarkable run of six NBA titles in eight years came to an end.

A Memorable Career

No matter how much trouble a player gets into, it seems there is always a team willing to take a chance on that person if they think it can help them win. Such was the case with Rodman. Despite his run-ins with coaches, referees, and the league office, he was signed to a contract by the Los Angeles Lakers in February 1999. He appeared in twenty-three games for the team before being waived that April.

In February 2000, the Dallas Mavericks signed Rodman to a $1 million contract. This time, he lasted just one month before being released by the club. Among other things, he alienated his teammates and owners with his criticism of the club. "[Owner] Mark Cuban wants to win," said Rodman, "but he's an owner, not a player. He doesn't need to be hanging around the players like he's a coach or something. . . . He needs to be the owner, step back and put people in who can get this team in the right direction."[80]

Dennis Rodman's fourteen-year NBA career was finally at an end. In addition to his five championship rings, he was an All-Star two times, the Defensive Player of the Year two times, and a member of the league's All-Defensive First Team six times. He is also the only player in history to win back-to-back NBA titles with two different teams.

Rodman's insistence on living his life according to his own rules has made him one of the most visible athletes of today. In addition to his countless fines and suspensions, he has attracted attention by, among other things, having an affair with the singer Madonna, marrying actress Carmen Electra, appearing at a book

Rodman on the court as a Los Angeles Laker. He joined the Lakers in 1999, only to be waived after twenty-three games.

Rodman appears at a book signing dressed as a bride. He has become famous for his colorful personality and flamboyant behavior.

signing dressed in a wedding gown, appearing in the 1997 movie *Double Time* with Jean Claude Van Damme, and having his own television show on MTV, *Rodman's World Tour.*

Rodman continues to remain in the public eye even though he no longer is an active player. The police are frequent visitors to his home when his partying disturbs his neighbors, and he has been the object of several lawsuits. He refuses to change his ways, however, insisting on following the beat of his own drum.

"The Worm" (a nickname given to him as a child because of the way he squirmed around while playing pinball) is generally regarded as the greatest rebounding forward in the history of the league. It is possible that another player may someday surpass him in that respect. One thing, however, is certain: There will never be another Dennis Rodman.

Chicago Bulls Achievements

Year-by-Year Records

Season	Coach	Finish	Wins	Losses	Playoff Wins	Losses
1966–67	Johnny Kerr	4th/Western Div.	33	48	0	3
1967–68	Johnny Kerr	4th/Western Div.	29	53	1	4
1968–69	Dick Motta	5th/Western Div.	33	49	–	–
1969–70	Dick Motta	T3rd/Western Div.	39	43	1	4
1970–71	Dick Motta	2nd/Midwest Div.	51	31	3	4
1971–72	Dick Motta	2nd/Midwest Div.	57	25	0	4
1972–73	Dick Motta	2nd/Midwest Div.	51	31	3	4
1973–74	Dick Motta	2nd/Midwest Div.	54	28	4	7
1974–75	Dick Motta	1st/Midwest Div.	47	35	7	6
1975–76	Dick Motta	4th/Midwest Div.	24	58	–	–
1976–77	Ed Badger	T2nd/Midwest Div.	44	38	1	2
1977–78	Ed Badger	3rd/Midwest Div.	40	42	–	–
1978–79	Larry Costello 20–36	5th/Midwest Div	31	51	–	–
	Scotty Robertson 11–15					
1979–80	Jerry Sloan	T3rd/Midwest Div.	30	52	–	–
1980–81	Jerry Sloan	2nd/Central Div.	45	37	2	4
1981–82	Jerry Sloan, 19–32	5th/Central Div.	34	48	–	–
	Phil Johnson, 0–1					
	Rod Thorn, 15–15					
1982–83	Paul Westhead	4th/Central Div.	28	54	–	–
1983–84	Kevin Loughery	5th/Central Div.	27	55	–	–
1984–85	Kevin Loughery	3rd/Central Div.	38	44	1	3
1985–86	Stan Albeck	4th/Central Div.	30	52	0	3
1986–87	Doug Collins	5th/Central Div.	40	42	0	3
1987–88	Doug Collins	T2nd/Central Div.	50	32	4	6

Season	Coach	Finish	Wins	Losses	Playoff Wins	Playoff Losses
1988–89	Doug Collins	5th/Central Div.	47	35	9	8
1989–90	Phil Jackson	2nd/Central Div.	55	27	10	6
1990–91	Phil Jackson	1st/Central Div.	61	21	15	2
1991–92	Phil Jackson	1st/Central Div.	67	15	15	7
1992–93	Phil Jackson	1st/Central Div.	57	25	15	4
1993–94	Phil Jackson	2nd/Central Div.	55	27	6	4
1994–95	Phil Jackson	3rd/Central Div.	47	35	5	5
1995–96	Phil Jackson	1st/Central Div.	72	10	15	3
1996–97	Phil Jackson	1st/Central Div.	69	13	15	4
1997–98	Phil Jackson	1st/Central Div.	62	20	15	6
1998–99	Tim Floyd	8th/Central Div.	13	37	–	–
1999–00	Tim Floyd	8th/Central Div.	17	65	–	–
2000–01	Tim Floyd	8th/Central Div.	15	67	–	–
Totals			1492	1345	147	106

NBA Most Valuable Player
(Maurice Podoloff Trophy)

Selected by vote of NBA players until 1976–80; by writers and broadcasters since 1980–81.

1987–88	Michael Jordan
1990–91	Michael Jordan
1991–92	Michael Jordan
1995–96	Michael Jordan
1997–98	Michael Jordan

IBM NBA Coach of the Year
(Red Auerbach Trophy)

Selected by writers and broadcasters.

1966–67	Johnny Kerr
1970–71	Dick Motta
1995–96	Phil Jackson

Schick NBA Rookie of the Year
(Eddie Gottlieb Trophy)

Selected by writers and broadcasters.

1984–85	Michael Jordan
1900–00	Elton Brand

NBA Executive of the Year

Selected by NBA executives for the Sporting News

1987–88	Jerry Krause
1995–96	Jerry Krause

NBA Defensive Player of the Year

Selected by writers and broadcasters.

1987–88   Michael Jordan

NBA Sixth Man Award

Selected by writers and broadcasters.

1995–96   Toni Kukoc

NBA Finals Most Valuable Player

Selected by writers and broadcasters.

1991	Michael Jordan
1992	Michael Jordan
1993	Michael Jordan
1996	Michael Jordan
1997	Michael Jordan
1998	Michael Jordan

Statistical Leaders
(Based on average per game.)
Scoring

Season	Points	
1986–87	37.1	Michael Jordan
1987–88	35.0	Michael Jordan
1988–89	32.5	Michael Jordan
1989–90	33.6	Michael Jordan
1990–91	31.5	Michael Jordan
1991–92	30.1	Michael Jordan
1992–93	32.6	Michael Jordan
1995–96	30.4	Michael Jordan
1996–97	29.6	Michael Jordan
1997–98	28.7	Michael Jordan

Field-Goal Percentage

Season	Points	
1980–81	.670	Artis Gilmore
1981–82	.652	Artis Gilmore

Free-Throw Percentage

Season	Points	
1970–71	.859	Chet Walker

Three-Point Field-Goal Percentage

Season	Points	
1994–95	.524	Steve Kerr

Minutes

Season	No.	
1986–87	3,281	Michael Jordan
1987–88	3,311	Michael Jordan
1988–89	3,255	Michael Jordan

Rebounding
(Based on average per game.)

Season	No.	
1995–96	14.9	Dennis Rodman
1996–97	16.1	Dennis Rodman
1997–98	15.0	Dennis Rodman

Assists

Season	No.	
1966–67	908	Guy Rodgers

Steals

Season	No.	
1987–88	3.16	Michael Jordan
1989–90	2.77	Michael Jordan
1992–93	2.83	Michael Jordan
1994–95	2.94	Scottie Pippen

Notes

Introduction: A Town Hungry for a Winner

1. Quoted in Alex Sachare, *The Chicago Bulls Encyclopedia*. Chicago, IL: Contemporary Books, 1998, p. xi.

Chapter 1: Making the Most of a Third Chance

2. Quoted in Sachare, *The Chicago Bulls Encyclopedia*, p. 5.
3. Quoted in Sachare, *The Chicago Bulls Encyclopedia*, p. 7.
4. Quoted in K.C. Johnson, "Getting Started: 1966–68," *Chicago Tribune*, February 17, 1997. www.chicagotribune.com/sports/bulls/ws/item/0,1308,472-474-480,00.html.
5. Quoted in Sachare, *The Chicago Bulls Encyclopedia*, p. 9.
6. Quoted in Sachare, *The Chicago Bulls Encyclopedia*, p. 14.
7. Quoted in K.C. Johnson, "Revolving Coaches: 1976–84," *Chicago Tribune*, February 17, 1997. www.chicagotribune.com/sports/bulls/ws/item/0,1308,472-475-483,00.html.
8. Quoted in Sachare, *The Chicago Bulls Encyclopedia*, pp. 23–24.
9. Quoted in Sachare, *The Chicago Bulls Encyclopedia*, p. 57.
10. Quoted in Sachare, *The Chicago Bulls Encyclopedia*, p. 64.
11. Quoted in Nancy Armour, "Chicago's Sellout Streak Ends at 610," *Detroit News*, November 8, 2000. www.detnews.com/2000/pistons/0011/08/sports-145707.htm.
12. Quoted in John Jackson, "Bulls," *The Sporting News Pro Basketball Yearbook 1999–2000*, p. 43.

Chapter 2: Chet Walker

13. Chet Walker, with Chris Messenger, *Long Time Coming*. New York: Grove Press, 1995, p. 18.
14. Walker, *Long Time Coming*, p. 52.
15. Quoted in Walker, *Long Time Coming*, p. 81.
16. "Q & A with Chet Walker," *Bulls.com*. www.nba.com/bulls/history/qa_with_chetwalker.html.

17. Quoted in "NBA Legends: Chet Walker," *National Basketball Association*. www.global.nba.com/history/walker_bio.html.
18. Quoted in "NBA Legends: Chet Walker."

Chapter 3: Bob Love

19. Robert Earl Love, with Mel Watkins, *The Bob Love Story: If It's Gonna Be, It's Up to Me*. Chicago, IL: Contemporary Books, 2000, p. 4.
20. Quoted in Love, *The Bob Love Story*, p. 32.
21. Quoted in Love, *The Bob Love Story*, pp. 52–53.
22. Quoted in Love, *The Bob Love Story*, p. 111.
23. Quoted in Barry Dalton, "Bulls Leading Scorer Shares His Story," *Missouri School Boards' Association*. www.msbanet.org/archives/showme-education/fall98/love.htm.
24. Quoted in Love, *The Bob Love Story*, p. 144.
25. Quoted in Jim Huber, "A Love Story," *CNN/Sports Illustrated*, March 24, 2000. www.cnnsi.com/inside_game/jim_huber/news/2000/03/17/insidersportinglife_love.
26. Quoted in Love, *The Bob Love Story*, p. 154.
27. Love, *The Bob Love Story*, p. 195.

Chapter 4: Michael Jordan

28. Quoted in Sachare, *The Chicago Bulls Encyclopedia*, p. 169.
29. Quoted in Charles Moritz, ed., *Current Biography Yearbook: 1987*. New York: H.W. Wilson, 1987, p. 290.
30. Quoted in Janet Lowe, *Michael Jordan Speaks*. New York: John Wiley & Sons, 1999, p. 7.
31. Quoted in Larry Schwartz, "Michael Jordan Transcends Hoops," *ESPN*. www.espn.go.com/classic/biography/s/Jordan_Michael.html.
32. Quoted in Schwartz, "Michael Jordan Transcends Hoops."
33. Quoted in Moritz, *Current Biography Yearbook: 1987*, p. 291.
34. Quoted in Sachare, *The Chicago Bulls Encyclopedia*, p. 52.
35. Quoted in Sachare, *The Chicago Bulls Encyclopedia*, p. 31.
36. Quoted in Sachare, *The Chicago Bulls Encyclopedia*, p. 186.
37. Quoted in Lowe, *Michael Jordan Speaks*, p. 77.
38. Quoted in Sachare, *The Chicago Bulls Encyclopedia*, p. 187.
39. Quoted in Sachare, *The Chicago Bulls Encyclopedia*, p. 191.
40. Quoted in Sachare, *The Chicago Bulls Encyclopedia*, p. 193.

41. Quoted in Sachare, *The Chicago Bulls Encyclopedia*, p. 195.
42. Quoted in "It's Official: Jordan Retires," *USA Today*, November 15, 1999. www.usatoday.com/sports/basketball/skn/jordan04.htm.
43. Quoted in "It's Official: Jordan Retires."
44. Quoted in Marty Burns, "Jordan Will Return to the NBA 'For the Love of the Game,'" *CNN/Sports Illustrated*, September 10, 2001. www.sportsillustrated.cnn.com/inside_game/marty_burns/news/2001/09/10/burns_insider.

Chapter 5: Scottie Pippen

45. Quoted in Sachare, *The Chicago Bulls Encyclopedia*, p. 213.
46. Quoted in Leigh Montville, "Out of the Shadow," *Sports Illustrated*, February 24, 1992, p. 80.
47. Quoted in Montville, "Out of the Shadow," p. 80.
48. Quoted in Montville, "Out of the Shadow," p. 80.
49. Quoted in Judith Graham, ed., *Current Biography Yearbook: 1994*. New York: H.W. Wilson, 1994, p. 454.
50. Quoted in Graham, *Current Biography Yearbook: 1994*, p. 454.
51. Quoted in Graham, *Current Biography Yearbook: 1994*, p. 454.
52. Quoted in Sachare, *The Chicago Bulls Encyclopedia*, p. 50.
53. Quoted in Sachare, *The Chicago Bulls Encyclopedia*, p. 214.
54. Quoted in Graham, *Current Biography Yearbook: 1994*, p. 456.
55. Quoted in Sachare, *The Chicago Bulls Encyclopedia*, p. 216.

Chapter 6: Phil Jackson

56. Quoted in Judith Graham, ed., *Current Biography Yearbook: 1992*. New York: H.W. Wilson, 1992, p. 288.
57. Phil Jackson and Charley Rosen, *More than a Game*. New York: Seven Stories Press, 2001, p. 21.
58. Quoted in Graham, *Current Biography Yearbook: 1992*, p. 289.
59. Quoted in Graham, *Current Biography Yearbook: 1992*, p. 289.
60. Quoted in Graham, *Current Biography Yearbook: 1992*, p. 288.
61. Quoted in Graham, *Current Biography Yearbook: 1992*, p. 289.
62. Quoted in Graham, *Current Biography Yearbook: 1992*, p. 289.
63. Quoted in Sachare, *The Chicago Bulls Encyclopedia*, p. 136.
64. Quoted in Graham, *Current Biography Yearbook: 1992*, p. 290.

65. Quoted in Sachare, *The Chicago Bulls Encyclopedia*, p. 49.
66. Quoted in Sachare, *The Chicago Bulls Encyclopedia*, p. 138.
67. Quoted in Charley Rosen, "No More Bull," *Cigar Aficionado*, September/October 1998. www.cigaraficionado.com/Cigar/Aficionado/people/fe1098.html.
68. Quoted in Rosen, "No More Bull."
69. Quoted in "Cool Under Pressure," *CNN*, June 12, 2000. www.fyi.cnn.com/2000/fyi/news/06/12/phil.jackson.ap.

Chapter 7: Dennis Rodman

70. Quoted in Dan Bickley, *No Bull: The Unauthorized Biography of Dennis Rodman*. New York: St. Martin's Press, 1997, p. 4.
71. Quoted in Bickley, *No Bull*, p. 18.
72. Quoted in Bickley, *No Bull*, p. 20.
73. Quoted in "What Makes Rodman Tick?" *Jet*, May 24, 1999. www.findarticles.com/cf_0/m1355/25_95/54757764/print.jhtml.
74. Quoted in Bickley, *No Bull*, p. 25.
75. Quoted in Bickley, *No Bull*, p. 54.
76. Quoted in Bickley, *No Bull*, p. 107.
77. Quoted in Bickley, *No Bull*, p. 162.
78. Quoted in Rosen, "No More Bull."
79. Quoted in Bickley, *No Bull*, p. 169.
80. Quoted in Bart Hubbuch, "Mavericks Release Rodman," *Dallas Morning News*, March 9, 2000. www.rodmanarchive.com/1col-20000309.html.

For Further Reading

Phil Jackson and Hugh Delahanty, *Sacred Hoops*. New York: Hyperion, 1995. An inside look at the basketball philosophy of the former Zen master head coach of the Chicago Bulls.

Roland Lazenby, *Blood on the Horns*. Lenexa, KS: Addax Publishing, 1998. The inside story of the breakup of the Chicago Bulls dynasty.

———, *Mindgames: Phil Jackson's Long Strange Journey*. New York: McGraw-Hill, 2000. The story of Phil Jackson's remarkable rise to the top of the NBA coaching hierarchy.

Dennis Rodman, *Bad as I Wanna Be*. New York: Delacorte Press, 1996. The autobiography of the NBA's most outrageous player.

Dennis Rodman, with Michael Silver, *Walk on the Wild Side*. New York: Delacorte Press, 1997. Another volume of ramblings from basketball's bad boy.

Sam Smith, *The Jordan Rules: The Inside Story of a Turbulent Season with Michael Jordan and the Chicago Bulls*. New York: Simon & Schuster, 1992. A penetrating look at Michael Jordan and the Chicago Bulls' 1990–1991 championship season.

Works Consulted

Books

Dan Bickley, *No Bull: The Unauthorized Biography of Dennis Rodman.* New York: St. Martin's Press, 1997. A chronicle of the life of basketball's bad boy, Dennis Rodman.

Judith Graham, ed., *Current Biography Yearbook: 1992.* New York: H.W. Wilson, 1992. Library volume that contains all of the biographies published in the *Current Biography* magazine in 1992, including Phil Jackson's.

————, *Current Biography Yearbook: 1994.* New York: H.W. Wilson, 1994. Library volume that contains all of the biographies published in the *Current Biography* magazine in 1994, including Scottie Pippen's.

David Halberstam, *Playing for Keeps.* New York: Broadway Books, 2000. The life of basketball's greatest player, Michael Jordan, as chronicled by a Pulitzer Prize–winning author.

Phil Jackson and Charley Rosen, *More than a Game.* New York: Seven Stories Press, 2001. Jackson's book explores the nuances of the game of basketball and the triangle offense.

Robert Earl Love, with Mel Watkins, *The Bob Love Story: If It's Gonna Be, It's Up to Me.* Chicago, IL: Contemporary Books, 2000. The inspirational life story of the All-Star forward of the Chicago Bulls.

Janet Lowe, *Michael Jordan Speaks.* New York: John Wiley & Sons, 1999. A collection of quotes by the world's most recognized sports celebrity.

Charles Moritz, ed., *Current Biography Yearbook: 1987.* New York: H.W. Wilson, 1987. Library volume that contains all of the biographies published in the *Current Biography* magazine in 1987, including Michael Jordan's.

Alex Sachare, *The Chicago Bulls Encyclopedia.* Chicago, IL: Contemporary Books, 1998. This valuable reference for Bulls fans has articles on Chicago history, memorable moments, rivalries, coaches, arenas, players, and owners, plus a comprehensive reference section.

Chet Walker, with Chris Messenger, *Long Time Coming*. New York: Grove Press, 1995. The autobiography of one of the first black athletes to gain celebrity status on the basketball court.

Periodicals

Frank Deford, "Father Phil," *Sports Illustrated*, November 1, 1999.

Richard Hoffer, "Sitting Bull," *Sports Illustrated*, May 27, 1996.

Johnette Howard, "Year of the Worm," *National Sports Daily*, May 20, 1990.

John Jackson, "Bulls," *The Sporting News Pro Basketball Yearbook 1999–2000.*

Jack McCallum, "For Whom the Bulls Toil," *Sports Illustrated*, November 11, 1991.

Leigh Montville, "Out of the Shadow," *Sports Illustrated*, February 24, 1992.

S.L. Price, "No Babe in the Woods," *Sports Illustrated*, December 13, 1999.

Peter Richmond, "Phil Jackson Then and Now," *National Sports Daily*, April 29, 1990.

Michael Silver, "Rodman Unchained," *Sports Illustrated*, May 29, 1995.

Joel Stein, "Michael Jordan: The End of the Line?" *Time*, June 22, 1998.

Rick Telander, "Demolition Man," *Sports Illustrated*, November 8, 1993.

Steve Wulf, "Cunning of the Bulls," *Time*, April 22, 1996.

Internet Sources

Nancy Armour, "Chicago's Sellout Streak Ends at 610," *Detroit News*, November 8, 2000. www.detnews.com/2000/pistons/0011/08/sports-145707.htm.

Marty Burns, "Jordan Will Return to the NBA 'For the Love of the Game,'" *CNN/Sports Illustrated*, September 10, 2001. www.sports

illustrated.cnn.com/inside_game/marty_burns/news/2001/0
9/10/burns_insider.

"Cool Under Pressure," *CNN*, June 12, 2000. www.fyi.cnn.
com/2000/fyi/news/06/12/phil.jackson.ap.

Barry Dalton, "Bulls Leading Scorer Shares His Story," *Missouri
School Boards' Association.* www.msbanet.org/archives/show
me-education/fall98/love.htm.

Bart Hubbuch, "Mavericks Release Rodman," *Dallas Morning News,*
March 9, 2000. www.rodmanarchive.com/1col-20000309.html.

Jim Huber, "A Love Story," *CNN/Sports Illustrated,* March 24,
2000. www.cnnsi.com/inside_game/jim_huber/news/2000/
03/17/insidersportinglife_love.

"It's Official: Jordan Retires," *USA Today,* November 15, 1999.
www.usatoday.com/sports/basketball/skn/jordan04.htm.

K.C. Johnson, "Getting Started: 1966–68," *Chicago Tribune,*
February 17, 1997. www.chicagotribune.com/sports/bulls/
ws/item/0,1308,472-474-480,00.html.

———, "Revolving Coaches: 1976–84," *Chicago Tribune,* February 17, 1997. www.chicagotribune.com/sports/bulls/ws/
item/0,1308,472-475-483,00.html.

"NBA Legends: Chet Walker," *National Basketball Association.*
www.global.nba.com/history/walker_bio.html.

"Q & A with Chet Walker," *Bulls.com.* www.nba.com/bulls/
history/qa_with_chetwalker.html

Charley Rosen, "No More Bull," *Cigar Aficionado,* September/Oc-
tober 1998. www.cigaraficionado.com/Cigar/Aficionado/
people/fe1098.html.

Larry Schwartz, "Michael Jordan Transcends Hoops," *ESPN.*
www.espn.go.com/classic/biography/s/Jordan_Michael.html.

"What Makes Rodman Tick?" *Jet,* May 24, 1999. www.findarticles.
com/cf_0/m1355/25_95/54757764/print.jhtml.

Website

National Basketball Association (www.nba.com). This is the
official website of the National Basketball Association.

Index

Picture Credits

About the Author

John F. Grabowski is a native of Brooklyn, New York. He holds a bachelor's degree in psychology from City College of New York and a master's degree in educational psychology from Teacher's College, Columbia University. He has been a teacher for thirty-three years, as well as a freelance writer, specializing in the fields of sports, education, and comedy. His body of published work includes thirty-five books; a nationally syndicated sports column; consultation on several math textbooks; articles for newspapers, magazines, and the programs of professional sports teams; and comedy material sold to Jay Leno, Joan Rivers, Yakov Smirnoff, and numerous other comics. He and his wife, Patricia, live in Staten Island with their daughter, Elizabeth.